MW01612002

THE APUSH CRUNCHER

A Guide for Passing the AP American History Exam

with Ease

Dr. Juan R. Céspedes, Ph.D.

TABLE OF CONTENTS   3

Novus Mundus Publishing

Introduction

Dear "Nervous Nelson" or "Nervous Nellie":

First and foremost...relax. The Advanced Placement United States History exam (hereinafter referred to as the "APUSH" exam) *is extremely doable*. I know this from personal experience, and I have been teaching for over thirty years. *This book has been carefully designed to give you the opportunity to score well on the exam.* How well? Unsurprisingly, that naturally depends on you. But if you put your heart into it you should score at least a 4 or higher, depending on the review time you allot. This is "quality" review time, what students refer in everyday language as "crunch time". Hence, the title of this guide for the APUSH exam. As human beings, it is normal while studying to have breaks and get up and stretch, have something to eat, etc. However, if after studying for 15 minutes you take a break which lasts 45 minutes, who is fooling whom? Pace yourself according to how much time you have before the exam, and focus. You can do it, millions of students have.

The APUSH Exam - What to Expect

The APUSH exam is approximately three hours and 5 minutes long and has two parts — a multiple choice section and an essay/free response section. Each section is worth 50% of the final exam grade. Let's examine exactly how the College Board (2013) breaks down the exam:

Section I: Multiple Choice — *80 questions; 55 minutes*

The portion of questions covering each time period is:

- *History through 1789 (20%)*

- *1790–1914 (45%)*

- *1915–Present (35%)*

Within those time periods, the portion of multiple choice questions covering each course theme is:

- *Political Institutions, behavior, and public policy (35%)*

- *Social and cultural developments (40%)*

- *Diplomacy and international relations (15%)*

- *Economic developments (10%)*

A substantial number of the social and economic history questions deal with such traditional topics as the impact of legislation on social groups and the economy, or the pressures brought to bear on the political process by social and economic developments.

Total scores on the multiple-choice section are based on the number of questions answered correctly. Points are not deducted for incorrect answers and no points are awarded for unanswered questions.

Section II: Free Response — *3 questions; 1 hour and 55 minutes plus a mandatory 15 minute reading period*

The free-response section covers the period from the first European explorations of the Americas to 1980.

- **Part A:** *1 Document Based Question (DBQ); 45 minutes*

  ○ *This section tests your ability to analyze and synthesize historical data and assess verbal, quantitative, or pictorial materials as historical evidence.*

  ○ *You will assess the value of a variety of documents and relate them to a historical period or theme to demonstrate knowledge of major periods and issues.*

  ○ *Documents will vary in length and format and may include charts, graphs, cartoons, and pictures, as well as written materials.*

- **Parts B:** *2 Standard Essay Questions; 70 minutes*

  ○ *The standard essay questions may require you to relate developments in different areas (e.g., the political implications of an economic issue); analyze common themes in different time periods (e.g., the concept of national interest in United States foreign policy); or compare individual or group experiences that reflect socioeconomic, ethnic, racial, or gender differences (e.g., social mobility and cultural pluralism).*

Essays will be graded on the strength of the thesis developed, the quality of the historical argument, and the evidence used to support your argument, rather than on the factual information per se.

In the free response section, Part A is worth 45% and Parts B is worth 55% of your free response score.

Tips to Greatly Improve Your Performance

Here are some tips that have been repeatedly shown to significantly improve your performance on the exam:

1. Multiple Choice: Time allotted and the Test Booklet

As previously mentioned, you have 55 minutes to answer 80 multiple choice questions. That gives you approximately 40 seconds per question. Therefore, you don't have time to waste. The best use of your time is spent by answering the questions you know best first, *and then* eliminating obvious wrong choices as you go through the remaining questions. You may write on the test booklet to keep track. Draw a line through the answers you know are wrong. Circle or otherwise indicate an unanswered question that you skipped so you can return to it later before the test ends.

2. Guessing in the Multiple Choice Section is Allowed

There are no additional point penalties for guessing. Therefore, eliminate as many options as possible, *then guess!*

3. Key Words Help in Determining Answers

Pay close attention to key words such as "always", "not", and "except", as they are of obvious importance in determining the correct answer. Look carefully at the wording of the question as well. There may be more than one answers which is *basically* correct, bit *one* answer is *the best* and thus the intended choice.

4. General Tips for Writing the Essay

Write with a "voice" which has an authorial presence. By a writer's "voice", is meant the sense the reader gets from the person writing the prose. In other words, write with authority on the subject. Take a definite stand in your answers. The first two or three sentences should succinctly state your thesis, and the rest of the essay should support the thesis.

5. Data Deluge Shouldn't be Subterfuge

Your essay should include *relevant* historical facts to prove your thesis. Do not try to awe the reader with a deluge of facts, it will not gain you extra points and may result in a lowering of your score. You also risk including incorrect information which would hurt your overall score.

6. Choosing Essay Questions

Standard essays - avoid broad survey questions. In spite of their appearance, they may be more difficult because of the breadth of knowledge required to answer them effectively. Writing a defendable thesis can present real problems for these types of questions.

7. Examining the Document-Based Questions (DBQs)

Read carefully each document presented. Come to a conclusion concerning the purpose, point of view, and the possible origin of each document. Feel free to circle, underline, or and make relevant historical notes in the margin on key points.

8. Using the Documents

You *do not* have to use all the documents presented to answer the DBQ. This is another case where depth is better than breath. Additionally, remember that time is not your friend. A good rule of thumb for adequately backing your thesis is to use 4 documents.

9. Answering the Document-Based Questions (DBQs)

Make sure to answer all parts of the question. It is advisable to quickly go over each part and reword as needed.

10. Physically Preparing for the Exam

Eat a healthy dinner the night before the exam, get a good night's sleep, and eat a good breakfast the morning of the exam.

Remember that the best advice in the world is useless, unless put into practice. *Use the above tips!*

The Subject Matter

Notice that this book has a shortened version of each historical topic, then refers you to an appendix if you need to brush-up on more information. Feel better about the exam? Now, let's get to the subject matter that will be covered on the exam.

[Image 1: Christopher Columbus, painting by Sebastiano del Piombo]

The First Inhabitants of the Americas

The first "Americans" were hunter gatherers who crossed the Bering Strait from Asia at least 12,000 to 15,000 years ago. An estimated two million, or more, of these peoples constituted the indigenous tribes living in the land that was to become the United States by the time Christopher Columbus completed his voyage to the New World in 1492.

Exploration and Settlement

European settlements sprang up in the latter part of the 16th century, following the initial exploration of the American coasts by the English, Spanish, Portuguese, French, and Dutch sea captains which started in late 15th century. In 1565 the Spanish established the first permanent settlement at St. Augustine, in what would one day become the state of Florida, and in 1599 another settlement in New Mexico. During the early 17th century the English were also competing for the New World, and founded Jamestown in the Colony of Virginia in 1607, and in present-day Massachusetts founded Plymouth Colony in 1620. A settlement in Fort

Orange, now Albany, New York, was established by the Dutch in 1624, New Amsterdam, now New York City, in 1626, and at Bergen, now part of Jersey City, New Jersey, in 1660. The Dutch also conquered New Sweden, the Swedish colony in Delaware and New Jersey, in 1655. However, nine years later the English subsequently monopolized the settlement of the East Coast, except for Florida (where Spanish rule prevailed until 1821), by seizing this New Netherlands Colony. Until the 19th century Arizona, California, Texas, and New Mexico were also part of the Spanish empire In the Southwest. The French established a few settlements and trading posts, but never established effective control in the area south of present-day Canada, known today as the Great Lakes. However, the thriving port city of New Orleans was one of the few areas where an active colonial policy was pursued by France.

From the founding of its first settlement in Jamestown to the start of the American Revolutionary War more than 150 years later, mercantilist policy was the primary means by which the British crown governed its American colonies: benefitting the 'mother country' economically was the *raison d'être* for the colonies. Raw materials would be shipped from the colonies in exchange for manufactured goods. Especially valued by the British was the lumber, tobacco, indigo, furs, rice, grain, and fish produced by the colonies, relying on the black slave labor of the southern colonies.

Until the end of the French and Indian War (1745–63: which resulted in the loss of French Canada to the British) the colonies enjoyed a large measure of autonomy (see Appendix 1: "French and Indian Wars"). In an effort to prevent trouble with the indigenous tribes, in 1763 the crown prohibited the establishment of settlements beyond the Appalachians by American colonists. Heavy expenditures obliged London to decree that the colonials should be responsible for their own defense, and so the British government passed a series of taxes to provide funds for that purpose. However, soon the political discourse grew to become one of local authority versus imperial mandate, as colonial insistence on having direct representation in the British parliament, prior to any consideration for taxation ("no taxation without representation" became a popular slogan in the thirteen colonies during the 1750-1760s, and one of the major causes of the American Revolutionary War).

Widening Intellectual and Cultural Differences

Also serving to separate the colonies from the mother country were widening intellectual and cultural differences. Changes in the colonists' attitudes and outlook occurred, evolving from their self-governance and remoteness from English traditions while living on the edge of the wilderness. The crown's efforts to diminish the power of colonial legislatures heralded an unavoidable antagonism between the colonies and the mother country, especially when one considers the previous "benign neglect" of mercantilist governance and the colonial's long tradition of almost complete self-government.

In 1773 the citizens of Massachusetts, dressed as Mohawks (a disguise which was intended to fool no one), protested a tax on tea by dumping into Boston harbor an entire cargo of belonging to the East India Company. King George III felt compelled to act. Punitive measures were enacted in defense of his authority as monarch, as well as in defense of private property. These measures were referred to as the "Intolerable Acts" by the colonists—and they attacked the very foundations of fairness and self-governance cherished by the colonials.

[Image 2: Colonial kitchen with woman spinning, an engraving. 1885]

The First Continental Congress and Independence

In response to the Intolerable Acts, delegates from 12 of the 13 colonies (Georgia was not represented) convened the First Continental Congress, which met in Philadelphia in September 1774. In addition to organizing a militia, the delegates proposed a general boycott of English merchandise. On 19 April 1775, the British marched to Concord, Massachusetts, and destroyed the supplies assembled by the colonists there. In nearby Lexington, American "minutemen" assembled that morning on the green and fired "the shot heard round the world" starting the Revolutionary war. The British infantry extracted themselves and fought their way back to Boston.

[Image 3: The Second Continental Congress voting independence. Author unknown. U.S. Constitution Sesquicentennial Commission. (1935 - ca. 12/31/1939)]

As the Second Continental Congress assembled in Philadelphia on 10 May 1775 (this time including Georgia), voices in favor of conciliation were raised, but all hopes for peace vanished with the news of the Restraining Act. The Act, passed on 30 March 1775, denied the colonists the right to trade with countries outside the British Empire. To the colonists, it represented economic servitude. With George Washington appointed commander in chief of the Continental Army, independence was declared on 4 July 1776 by the 13 American colonies, justifying their right to rebel on the theory of natural rights expounded by philosophers such as John Locke.

The first significant battle, Bunker Hill—fought mostly on and around Breed's Hill—between the Americans and the British occurred near Boston on 17 June 1775. It was a Pyrrhic victory for the British, who suffered heavy losses: 226 killed (including a notably large number of officers including General Warren) and over 800 wounded. Throughout the coast numerous battles were to follow, with the British unable to inflict a decisive defeat on Washington, although they seized and held the principal cities. Eventually the balance was tipped in favor of the Americans by the entry of France into the conflict. The goal of the French was to weaken Britain militarily, and to exact revenge for the defeat in the the Seven Years' War. On 19 October 1781, the British commander, Cornwallis, surrendered his army at Yorktown. He had no other options; besieged by American and French forces on land, and cut off from reinforcements by sea by the French fleet—General Charles O'Hara, carried Cornwallis' sword to the American and French commanders. As the 8,000 British and Hessian troops marched out to surrender, the British band played the song "The World Turned Upside Down." Although the war continued on the high seas and in other theaters, the Patriot victory effectively ended the fight for independence. Formal negotiations began in 1782, and on 3 September 1783, the Treaty of Paris was signed, with the British recognizing the sovereignty of the United States after eight years of war (see Appendix 2: "American Revolutionary War").

The Articles of Confederation

The Articles of Confederation, the first national governing document uniting the 13 original colonies, revealed all the suspicions and distrust that Americans had about a strong centralized government. Each state was in effect a sovereign nation, Congress was denied the power to regulate commerce or tax, and an approval by 9 of the 13 states was required before it was permitted to carry out many of the powers it *was* authorized to exercise. The hardships of a postwar economic downturn aggravated popular dissatisfaction with the Articles of Confederation, and by 1787, the same year that Congress dealt with the organization of new territories and states on the frontier by passing the Northwest Ordinance, a convention to revise the Articles assembled in Philadelphia.

The convention met from 25 May to 17 September 1787, adopted what became the present Constitution of the United States, and the power of the central government was greatly increased at the expense of the individual states. The most heated disputes revolved around the composition and election of the Senate, the definition of "proportional representation", the selection and powers of the president, whether to allow the abolition of the slave trade, and issues concerning personal freedoms. Ratification was accomplished with the understanding that the constitution would be amended to include a Bill of Rights guaranteeing certain unalienable rights —including the freedom of speech, a free press, freedom from unreasonable search and seizure, freedom of assembly, and the right to an impartial jury and speedy trial. The first 10 amendments to the constitution assured these rights, and were adopted on 5 December 1791. Unsurprisingly, this 18th century document provided for limited suffrage and recognized slavery (twenty-five of the convention's 55 delegates owned slaves—Congress would have the power to ban the international slave trade after 20 years—not until 1808). On 30 April 1789, George Washington was inaugurated as the first president of the United States.

The credit of the new nation was bolstered during Washington's administration by acts providing for a revenue tariff and an excise tax on Whiskey. Opposition to the tax on whiskey sparked the Whiskey Rebellion. The tax was a part of Alexander Hamilton's (then Treasury Secretary) program to fund the war debt. On Washington's orders, the rebellion was suppressed in 1794. Also implemented were Hamilton's proposals for permitting the national government to assume the debts of the states and funding the domestic and foreign debt. Hamilton, the founder of the Federalist Party, also created the first national bank. Opposition to Hamiltonian policies, which tended to favor the commercial interests of the Northeast, as well as opposition to the bank, led to the creation of the Democratic-Republicans, an anti-Federalist party.

[Image 4: The "Committee of Five" that drafted the U.S. Declaration of Independence. Composite of paintings of various authors. Left to right: Roger Sherman, Benjamin Franklin, Thomas Jefferson, John Adams, Robert R. Livingston.]

The Federalist Party

The ideological divide between Democratic-Republicans and the Federalists was significant. Although the Democratic-Republicans condemned the violence of the French revolution, they applauded the overthrow of the French monarchy and likened it to the American struggle against tyranny. Their ideological opposite was the Federalist Party (Washington was a member), which regarded the French Revolution as a threat to property and personal security. This split into two adversarial camps was the first manifestation of the two-party system, the primary and dominant characteristic of the political life of the United States. Although they share important similarities, Jefferson's Democratic-Republicans should not be confused with the present-ay Republican Party, formed in 1854 (see Appendix 3: "Jeffersonian Principles").

The Election of 1800

The results of the election of 1800 was the victory of Jefferson over Federalist president John Adams, Washington's successor. The unpopularity of the Alien and Sedition Acts (1798), outlawing open dissent and severely limiting free speech, was a key factor in Jefferson's victory. Jefferson purchased the Louisiana Territory from France in 1803, which included 828,000 acres west of the Mississippi and encompassed 15 present US states and two Canadian provinces. Mapping and exploration of the newly acquired territory began almost immediately through the expeditions of Meriwether Lewis and William Clark (they also collected information on the indigenous peoples and scientific information). The landmark case of Marbury vs. Madison, under Chief Justice John Marshall, established the doctrine of judicial review by the Supreme Court and the principle of federal supremacy in conflicts with the states.

During the second term of Jefferson's presidency, the United States experienced worsening relations with Britain, as the United States tried to remain neutral in the midst of the Napoleonic Wars in Europe. The administration passed the Embargo Act of 1807 in response to the seizures of US ships and the impressment of US seamen by the British navy. After the repeal of the Embargo Act in 1809, the British continued with the seizure of ships and impressment of seamen, and was the prominent reason for the War of 1812 during the presidency of James Madison. However, an additional factor in the War of 1812 was the Westerners' coveting of southern Canadian lands as potential US territory. The war was essentially a draw. British successes on land, which included the torching of the White House, were countered by unexpected naval victories by the Americans. The war ended with the Treaty of Ghent, signed 24 December 1814. The treaty provided for no territorial changes and made no mention of the impressment issue. With the defeat of Napoleon in 1815 further maritime conflict with Britain ended (see Appendix 4: "War of 1812").

Westward expansion and domestic problems now the became the nation's primary focus. Textiles and other industries flourished in New England because during the war the United States had been cut off from its normal sources of manufactured goods in Great Britain. In 1816 Congress adopted a high-tariff policy to protect these infant industries.

[Image 5; Portrait of Thomas Jefferson by Rembrandt Peale, 1800.]

n the late 1810s and the 1820s three events held great consequence for the country's future. In 1817 the federal government began the forcible resettling of the indigenous peoples (Native Americans), whose populations were already markedly reduced by war and disease, into what subsequently became known as "Indian Territory" (now the area of Oklahoma). Those tribes who were not forced to relocate were restricted to reservations. Next, an attempt to settle the divisive and volatile question of slavery in the new territories was made with the Missouri Compromise of 1820. It banned slavery in territories to the west that lay north of the parallel 36°30', but provided for admission of Missouri into the Union as a slave state. Finally, in 1823 President James Monroe asserted that the

Western Hemisphere was closed to colonization by European powers, as a result of threats by France and Spain to reestablish colonial rule in the now independent republics of Latin America. Consequently, the "Monroe Doctrine" proclaimed that efforts by such powers to reacquire territories whose sovereignty the United States had recognized would be regarded as a hostile act (see Appendix 5: "Monroe Doctrine").

The Growth of Manufacturing

From the 1820s to the outbreak of the Civil War in 1861, technological advances and new inventions accelerated the growth of manufacturing, mainly in the North. Westward migration was accompanied with an expansion in farming. With the invention of the Cotton Gin by Eli Whitney in 1793, the South determined that its future lay in the cultivation of cotton. The cotton gin greatly simplified the problems of production, and the expansion of the textile industry in New England and Great Britain secured an abiding market for cotton. Thus, the South stayed a fundamentally agrarian economy during the first half of the 19th century, its society based increasingly on monoculture. Slavery became entrenched in the economy of the south, as large numbers of field laborers were required for cotton cultivation and harvesting.

The country's territorial growth and economic expansion was accompanied by a parallel growth in the construction of roads and canals. A canal-building boom was ushered in with the successful completion of the Erie Canal in 1825, linking the Atlantic with the Great Lakes. In the 1830s railroad building had begun in earnest, and by 1840, about 3,300 miles of track had been laid. In 1843, Samuel F. B. Morse built a telegraph system from Washington, DC, to Baltimore with the financial support of Congress, and thus commenced the modern telecommunications network for the nation. The earliest unionization efforts accompanied the establishment of the factory system, and in the North a laboring class developed.

A 'democratic revolution' was sparked as Western states admitted into the Union following the War of 1812 provided suffrage for free white males without property. Popular appeal became an important prerequisite for political candidates as states in the East began to broaden the franchise. The election of Tennessean Andrew Johnson to the presidency in 1828, an Indian fighter and military hero, resulted without a doubt from this widened democratic process. The United States by this time had a population of nearly 13 million inhabitants and consisted of 24 states.

The Relentless Westward Thrust

[Image 6: A covered wagon at the Texas Parks and Wildlife Expo 2007.]

Invariably, the United States was involved in a foreign conflict due to the relentless westward thrust of its population. An independent republic was established in 1836 by US settlers in Texas, as they revolted against Mexican rule. Relations between the government of Mexico and the United States worsened steadily as Texas was admitted in 1845 into the Union as a state. Although fraught with internal political struggles, Mexico was relatively united in refusing to recognize the independence of Texas. Boundary disputes arose, with the government of Antonio López de Santa Anna laying claim to territories as far north as the Nueces River, and the US claiming that the border was the Rio Grande. President James K. Polk had his *casus belli*, approved by Congress on 13 May 1846, when the Mexicans attacked a US patrol.

Outnumbered militarily, US forces captured Mexico City after a rapid advance, and on 2 February 1848, Mexico formally ended the struggle by signing the Treaty of Guadalupe Hidalgo on 2 February 1848. The treaty providing for the cession by Mexico of California and the territory of New Mexico to the United States (see Appendix 6: "Mexican-American War"). For $10 million, the United States acquired from Mexico large strips of land forming the balance of southern Arizona and New Mexico with the Gadsden Purchase of 1853. In 1846 a dispute with Britain over the Oregon Territory was ended by a treaty that established the 49th parallel as the border with Canada. Thereafter, the United States established itself as a Pacific as well as an Atlantic power.

Bleeding Kansas

[Image 7: Abolitionist John Brown, 1854]

The issue over slavery in the new territories was exacerbated by the country's Westward expansion. By 1840, the abolition or maintenance of slavery had become a passionate and often violent debate, as evidenced by the caning in Congress of Senator Charles Sumner, a Massachusetts antislavery Republican, by pro-slavery Representative Preston Brooks, a Democrat from South Carolina. There existed other movements for fundamental moral reform, which encompassed temperance, women's rights, universal education, and the amelioration of working class hardships. In 1849, a year after the discovery of gold had provoked a headlong gallop of new settlers to California, that 'free' territory—its constitution prohibited slavery—demanded to be admitted into the Union. In 1850 Kentucky Senator Henry Clay engineered a compromise in Congress providing for California's admission as a free state in return for various concessions to the South, including:

- Organization of the Utah and New Mexico territories without slavery provisions, giving the territorial populations the right to determine whether or not to allow slavery.

- In the District of Columbia, the prohibition of the slave trade, but not the ownership of slaves.

- A more stringent Fugitive Slave Act

- The establishment of state boundaries for Texas in exchange for federal payment of Texas's ten million dollar debt.

- A declaration by Congress that it did not have the authority to interfere with the interstate slave trade.

But there would be no settling the animosities dividing North and South. The question of slavery in the territories reached a crucial stage in 1854 with the Kansas-Nebraska Act, which repealed the Missouri Compromise, and left the question of slavery to be decided by the settlers of the new territories. Proslavery and antislavery settlers flooded into Kansas to try to influence the outcome of the decision. Violence erupted as both factions fought for control. Abolitionist John Brown led anti-slavery fighters in Kansas before his famed but ill-advised raid on Harpers Ferry. The clashes ensuing between northern and southern settlers in Kansas earned the territory the name "bleeding Kansas."

Lincoln's Election and Civil War

In 1860, two presidential candidates were offered by the Democratic Party, which was split along northern and southern lines. Abraham Lincoln was nominated by the relatively new Republican Party, which was organized in 1854 and was opposed to the expansion, if not the outright abolition, of slavery. Lincoln was able to carry the election in the electoral college, due to defections in the ranks of the Democrats, although he did not obtain a majority of the popular vote. Lincoln's election was seen as a threat to the ardent supporters of slavery, and provided a reason for immediate secession from the Union. Under the presidency of Jefferson Davis the seven slaveholding states of the Deep South—South Carolina, Mississippi, Florida, Alabama, Georgia, Louisiana, and Texas—seceded from the United States between December 1860 and February 1861, and formed a separate government known as the Confederate States of America. Eventually, eleven southern states seceded from the Union. Almost immediately, the confiscation of Federal property in the South was begun by the secessionists. On 12 April 1861, war was precipitated when the Confederates opened fire on Fort Sumter in the harbor of Charleston, South Carolina. Following the outbreak of hostilities, Arkansas, North Carolina, Virginia, and Tennessee joined the Confederacy. The Civil War had begun.

[Image 8: Abraham Lincoln, Republican candidate for the presidency, 1860.]

The war raged between the Confederate and Union forces for the next four years, largely in the territory of the southern states. Immense battles raged in places such as Shiloh (6–7 April, 1862), Fredericksburg (11–15 December, 1862), Chancellorsville (30 April– 6 May, 1863), Vicksburg (18 May– 4 July, 1863), Chickamauga (19–20 September, 1863) and in Virginia and Tennessee, where 40 percent of the 10,000 engagements of the war were fought. Confederate tactical genius General Robert E. Lee invaded Maryland in September 1862, but there he suffered a major loss at the Battle of Antietam, the bloodiest engagement of the war (23,000 soldiers were killed, wounded or missing after twelve hours of fierce combat on 17 September 1862).

The Union forces, suffering under poor generalship until the arrival of Ulysses S. Grant and William Tecumseh Sherman, finally prevailed, having superiority in manpower and resources. The Union Army was thrashed by Lee at Chancellorsville (30 April–6 May, 1863) and the Confederates invaded Pennsylvania, leading to the summital Battle of Gettysburg (1–3 July, 1863) in which Lee was forced to retreat to Virginia, never to invade the North again, and in which 50,000 men were either killed or wounded. A Union army took Atlanta, Georgia, on 2 September 1864; and the Confederate forces evacuated Richmond, Virginia, the Confederate capital, on the 2 April, 1865. With the Union holding much of the Confederacy in its hands, Confederate General Robert E. Lee surrendered to General Ulysses S. Grant at Appomattox Courthouse in Virginia on 9 April, 1865.

The human costs of the Civil War were staggering, Confederate dead were estimated at 250,000, including 94,000 killed in combat; on the Union side, 360,000 men died of various causes, including 110,000 killed in combat. The south was economically devastated, and an untold number of civilians also perished, primarily from disease and starvation (see Appendix 7: "Civil War").

The Outcomes of the Civil War

The Civil War brought about great changes in the nation's life. Lincoln's Emancipation Proclamation of 1863 initiated the freeing some four million slaves; soon after the war's end their liberation was completed by the 13th amendment to the Constitution. Only five days after Lee's surrender, Lincoln's compassionate plans for the reconstruction of the rebellious states were interrupted by his assassination at the hands of by John Wilkes Booth. The assassination was part of a conspiracy in which US Secretary of State William H. Seward was seriously wounded as well.

Union Army commanders governed the defeated South during the Reconstruction era (1865–1877), and for years afterward the consequential venomousness of southerners toward Republican rule and northerners, which freed and empowered blacks, persisted. Vice President Andrew Johnson, who succeeded Lincoln as president, attempted to implement Lincoln's policies of reconciliation, but after the assassination he was stringently opposed by Congressional Republican leaders who insisted on harsher treatment of the South. The divide between Johnson and Congress grew, and using the pretext that he had been negligent in carrying out an act of Congress, the House of Representatives voted for impeachment in 1868, but the conviction failed in the Senate by one vote and he remained in office. During Johnson's presidency Secretary of State William H. Seward negotiated the purchase of Alaska from Czarist Russia for $7.2 million (i.e., "Seward's Folly"). Russia, fearing that a war with Britain would allow the British to seize Alaska, was glad to sell.

Some southern whites attempted to regain political control of their states through the formation of clandestine organizations like the Ku Klux Klan, which terrorized their opponents and prevented blacks from exercising their right to vote. Whites had reestablished their sociopolitical dominance over blacks in the South by the end of the Reconstruction era, and began to enforce patterns of segregation in education and local laws (i.e., "black codes") that were to last for nearly another century (see Appendix 8: "Reconstruction").

The Decades Following the Civil War

For most of the southern states, the decades following the Civil War were ones in which rural whites as well as blacks were reduced to sharecropper status due to the war's economic devastation. However, in the North a period of abundant economic growth began. Railroad networks blossomed throughout the country (by 1869 the Transcontinental Railroad opened for through traffic), corporations multiplied and expanded, and the western lands remaining were rapidly peopled and settled. The age of big business tycoons (or "robber barons" to their critics) dawned with super-entrepreneurs like Andrew Carnegie, John D. Rockefeller, Jay Gould, and J. P. Morgan. New York, Chicago, and Pittsburgh emerged as the nation's great industrial centers, as heavy manufacturing developed. The Knights of Labor, the largest and one of the most important American labor organizations, founded in 1869, engaged in numerous work-stoppages and strikes, and conflicts between strikers and strikebreakers were common and violent. The American Federation of Labor, an alliance of craft unions founded in 1886, established a nationwide system of unionism that remained highly powerful and influential for decades. Although woman's suffrage was not enacted in the US until 1920, during this period the woman's rights movement led by suffragettes like Elizabeth Cady Stanton, Lucretia Mott, and Lucy Stone actively organized to secure the vote. Groups such as the National Audubon Society (named in honor of naturalist and ornithologist John J. Audubon), outraged by the depletion of wildlife and forests in the West, pressed for the conservation of natural resources.

Due to the accelerated westward expansion, additional room for millions of immigrants from Europe was made during the latter half of the 19th century. By the year 1900, the country's population had increased to more than 76 million inhabitants. The federal government forced the indigenous tribes west of the Mississippi to give up vast tracts of land to the whites, as prospectors and homesteaders settlers "tamed the frontier". This white migration precipitated a series of wars with various tribes, such as the Battle of Little Bighorn (i.e., "Custer's Last Stand", Montana, 1876), Battle of Big Hole (1877, Montana) the Meeker Massacre (1879, Colorado), and the Battle of Sugar Point (1898, Minnesota; the last Medal of Honor given for Indian Wars Campaigns was awarded to Pvt. Oscar Burkard of 3rd US Infantry Regiment). By 1890, only 250,000 native Americans remained in the United States, practically all of them residing unwillingly on reservations.

The 1890s

The end of the "Gilded Age" also marked the end of the expansion of the continental frontier for settlement, and the commencement of American overseas expansion. By 1892, American sugar planters in the Hawaiian islands had become politically formidable enough to bring about the overthrow of the native monarchy of Queen Lili'uokalani and establish a republic under the provisional government of Sanford B. Dole, which in 1898, at its own behest, was annexed as a territory by the United States (Hawaii will not be admitted into the Union as a state until 21 August, 1959).

Aroused by the yellow journalism of a lurid press and expansionist sentiments, the sympathies of the United States lay with the Cuban nationalists who had been battling for independence from Spain. The Cubans had fought three wars attempting to gain their independence; the Ten Years' War (1868–1878), the Little War (1879–1880), and the final war

(1895-1898) whose concluding three months escalated into what became the Spanish American War. The worsening relations between the US and the Spanish government climaxed with the sinking of the USS *Maine* in Havana Harbor. While the cause of the tragedy was undetermined, American popular opinion blamed Spain, and President William McKinley declared war on Spain on 25 April 1898 (with Madrid declaring war first). The power of the US Navy proved decisive, allowing American forces to disembark in Cuba and fight a Spanish garrison already weakened by the Cuban insurgents (i.e., *Mambises,* largely armed with machetes). As a result of the short conflict the 1898 Treaty of Paris was signed, whereby the United States was allowed temporary control of Cuba, and ceded indefinite colonial authority over Puerto Rico, Guam, and the Philippine Islands (see Appendix 9: "Spanish-American War"). In 1902 the newly independent Republic of Cuba began a tradition of close economic and political ties with the United States, that critics saw as a virtual dependency, and that was to last until 1959. Some prominent Americans saw these imperialistic undertakings as a desertion of the long-established and respected doctrine of government by the consent of the governed.

[Image 9: Smartly dressed couple seated on an 1886-model bicycle for two. The South Portico of the White House, Washington, DC, in the background.]

With the increased expansion of large corporations came increasing protests against the vexatious policies of "big business" and its all-absorbing role in the economic life of the nation. Antitrust laws to control monopolistic business practices were passed and implemented by a movement that came to be called "progressivism". Two US presidents, Theodore "Teddy" Roosevelt (1901–1909), a Republican, and Woodrow Wilson (1913–1921), a Democrat, came to be closely identified with the progressivist movement. Roosevelt acquired an appreciable reputation as a "trustbuster". Wilson's program, became known as the "New Freedom", and called for reforms in banking, tariffs, and business procedures (see Appendix 10: "Progressivism"). Roosevelt's assertive style in foreign relations was called Big Stick Diplomacy, originating from his favorite phrase "Speak softly and carry a big stick, and you will go far." The Roosevelt Corollary to the Monroe Doctrine is a prime example of Big Stick diplomacy. The Roosevelt Administration secretly supported a coup to overthrow Colombia's government and grant Panamanian independence, so that the United States could build the Panama Canal. During Roosevelt's presidency, the United States started construction of the 42 mile canal, completed in 1914—an impressive Rooseveltian legacy.

World War I

[Image 10: A Renault Tank model WWI.]

US participation in World War I indicated the country's ascendancy as a world power. Sentiment in the United States was decidedly isolationist in the 1914 conflict between Germany, Austria-Hungary, and Turkey on one side (the Central Powers), and France, Britain, and Russia on the other (the Allies)—although a significant portion of the American populace sympathized with the French and the British. The Germans, struggling to overcome a British blockade, resorted to unrestricted submarine warfare, although in fairness both sides violated US maritime rights on the high seas.

On 6 April 1917, Congress declared war on Germany. Fighting since the summer of 1914, war weary Britain, France, and Russia welcomed news that fresh American troops and supplies would be directed toward the Allied war effort. Some four million US soldiers between the ages of 18 and 45 were trained through a national draft, of whom more than two million were sent overseas to France, arriving at the port of St. Nazaire. By late 1917, as the European armies were approaching exhaustion, US troops began to take part in the fighting on the western front, as units from the Army's First Division were assigned to Allied trenches in the Luneville sector near Nancy.

US intervention became a decisive factor in aiding the eventual victory of the Allies. In a series of epic battles in which US soldiers took increasing predominance, the Kaiser's forces were rolled back eastward, and in the autumn of 1918 Germany was compelled to sue for peace. On 11 AM, 11th of November, 1918, the fighting ended with an armistice of (see Appendix 11: "World War I"). President Wilson played a vital role in the composition of the Versailles peace treaty of 1919, which epitomized his vision of a League of Nations to preserve the peace, but the ratification of the treaty was prevented by the isolationist bloc in the Senate.

The 1920s

The United States had little desire remaining for foreign entanglements In the 1920s, or for reform at home. The Kellogg-Briand Pact of 1928, where the signatories promised not to use war to resolve their problems, represented an uncommon instance of idealism on the part of the US. The "roaring '20s" saw a great business boom, and the philosophy of the nation, as well as that of the Republican administrations from 1921 to 1933, was reflected in the observation "the business of America is business." The years 1923–24 bore witness to the Teapot Dome scandal, where Albert B. Fall, President Warren G. Harding's secretary of the interior, had secretly leased federal oil reserves in Wyoming and California to private oil companies in return for gifts and loans.

[Image 11: Mlle. Rhea seated with flask in garter on leg. Photograph made on 26 January 1926, during prohibition in the United States.]

The Depression of the 1930s

The most intense and most protracted economic depression the US had ever known was ushered in by the great stock market crash of October 1929. Personal savings were wiped out on a vast scale through a disastrous series of bank failures and corporate bankruptcies, and an estimated 12 million men and women were out of work by 1933. Overwhelmed private charities and local governments were the only venues for providing relief for the unemployed, and were unable to handle the enormous task.

Democrat Franklin D. Roosevelt's (FDR) inauguration on March 1933 opened a new chapter in US history, in which the federal government assumed a much greater role in the economic affairs of the nation. The Roosevelt administration assumed responsibility for alleviating the hardships of national unemployment and stimulating economic recovery, proposing to give the country a "New Deal".

Deficit spending was instituted and work projects created to remedy the public's distress. Various social programs designed to stimulate and develop the economy through federal intervention were inaugurated, such as the Social Security program. The National Labor Relations Act strengthened unions by established the right of employee organizations to engage in collective bargaining with employers. Membership in unions rapidly increased. The newly formed Congress of Industrial Organizations (CIO), which organized workers along industrial lines, challenged the dominance of the American Federation of Labor (AFL). Some economists believe that by raising wages and prices during an economic slump, FDR's New Deal policies lengthened the depression by as many as 7 years (see Appendix 12: "The New Deal").

[Image 12: The Great Depression. Breadlines:long line of people waiting to be fed: New York City: in the absence of substantial government relief programs during 1932, free food was distributed with private funds in some urban centers to large numbers of the unemployed. Author unknown. Circa February 1932.]

War Clouds - 7 December 1941

The great depression of the 1930s was international in nature, and some countries attempted to provide economic economic stimulus by building large armed forces and embarking on imperialistic expansion. World War II broke out in Europe during September 1939, following aggression by the totalitarian German, Italian, and Japanese governments. Disregarding a tradition dating back to Washington that no president should serve more than two terms, Roosevelt ran again for reelection In 1940. His Republican opponent, Wendell Willkie, was easily defeated. While campaigning, both candidates advocated providing all possible aid to the victims of aggression and increased rearmament.

[Image 13: An SBD Dauntless dropping its bomb. The SBD ("Scout Bomber Douglas") was the U.S. Navy's main carrier-borne scout plane and dive bomber from mid-1940 through mid-1944.]

Although attempting to remain 'neutral' while providing military aid to Britain, on 7 December 1941, the United States was thrust into the war by the surprise Japanese attack on the American fleet anchored at Pearl Harbor in Hawaii. The Axis Powers, the armed forces of Nazi Germany, its junior partner Fascist Italy, and Imperial Japan, were now arrayed over an immense theater of war against those of the Allies, the US, the Free

French, the British Commonwealth, and the USSR. The Nazi Wehrmacht was engaged in a bloody and gigantic struggle with the Soviet Union in Eastern Europe. Across the immense expanses of the Pacific Ocean, in Africa, in Asia, and in Western Europe, the armed forces of the US waged war. In 1943 Italy surrendered; in 1944 Germany was successfully invaded and defeated in May 1945; and the Japanese capitulated in August 1945 after the United States dropped the world's first atomic bombs on Hiroshima and Nagasaki (see Appendix 13: "World War II & the Postwar World"). On 4 July 1946, the US relinquished its sovereignty over the Philippines, and the islands became an independent republic. The US maintained ownership over most of its other Pacific possessions.

Vice President Harry S. Truman succeeded president Franklin D. Roosevelt, who had been elected to a fourth term in 1944, but died in April 1945 of a cerebral hemorrhage. The US became an important member of a new world organization, the United Nations, under the Truman administration. In order to stop the expansion of communism, the Truman administration embarked on a policy of "containment"; large scale programs of military aid and economic support to friendly nations battling communist subversion. Economic assistance became an outstanding characteristic of postwar foreign policy, as demonstrated by US aid to Greece and Turkey in 1948, and the Marshall Plan, intended to facilitate the economic recovery of Western Europe (see Appendix 14: "The Marshall Plan"). In 1949, the North Atlantic Treaty Organization was established as a defensive alliance among the nations of Western Europe and the United States against Soviet invasion. Scientific and technical aid to developing nations was afforded through Truman's Point Four program.

The North Korean Attack

The UN Security Council resolved that its members should proceed to the aid of South Korea following an attack by the forces of North Korea on 25 June 1950. President Truman immediately dispatched American naval, air, and ground forces to the conflict. An undeclared war followed, which an armistice eventually signed on 27 June 1953 brought to a halt (see Appendix 15: "Korean War").

In 1952, Republican Dwight D. Eisenhower, former supreme commander of all Allied forces in Europe during World War II, was elected president, thereby ending 20 years of Democratic presidential monopoly. Eisenhower, the most highly credentialed president of the 20th century, continued the Truman policy of containing the USSR, and threatened "massive retaliation" in the event of Soviet aggression. Cold War tensions were heightened between the world's two great nuclear powers over crises in Egypt, Berlin, the Congo, Hungary, the U-2 incident, and the islands of Quemoy and Matsu off the coast of China. Although the domestic policies of the Republicans were more conservative than those of the Democrats, the Eisenhower administration extended Social Security, public housing, and certain social and economic programs of the Roosevelt and Truman administrations. The early years of the Eisenhower administration were marked by Congressional investigations, arising in 1950, over alleged charges of Communist and other subversive activities in the United States. These charges were initiated by Republican Senator Joseph R. McCarthy of Wisconsin, who aroused much controversy with allegations that Communists had penetrated the Army, the Department of State, and other branches of government. This phenomenon became known as McCarthyism. New information obtained from files of the now defunct USSR and the Venona Intercepts—FBI recordings of Soviet embassy communications between 1944-1948—shows that the senator was essentially correct. Whether it was influencing US foreign policy or stealing atomic secrets, communist victories in the 1940s were fed by an incredibly vast influence and spy network. Even those who opposed McCarthy's investigations lent their support to the blacklisting of persons with left-wing backgrounds and the requirement of loyalty oaths by government officials.

The 1954 US Supreme Court's landmark decision in *Brown v. Board of Education of Topeka*, outlawing the segregation in public schools of whites and blacks, was a major event of the Eisenhower years. Desegregation proceeded slowly and painfully in the wake of this ruling. "Freedom rides," sit-ins, and similar expressions of nonviolent resistance by blacks and their sympathizers, led to a lessening of segregation practices in public facilities in the early 1960s. The Supreme Court in 1962 mandated the reapportionment of state and federal legislative districts according to the formula of "one person, one vote" under Chief Justice Earl Warren. It also established the duty of police officers to advise an accused person of their legal rights immediately upon arrest, and extended the rights of defendants in criminal trials to include provisions of a lawyer for an accused person unable to afford one at the expense of the public.

The Cold War

In the early 1960s, the Cold War heated up for John F. Kennedy, Eisenhower's Democratic successor, as Cuba aligned itself with the Soviet Union under the dictatorial régime of Fidel Castro. Eisenhower had been unable to counter the increasingly Marxist revolution in Cuba, but left the Kennedy Administration with well-conceived plans to topple Castro that would ultimately be known as the Bay of Pigs invasion, or *Playa Girón* to the Cuban exile community. By the time the invasion took place on 17 April 1961, Kennedy had so immensely changed the original plans (starting with the elimination of all air strikes except the first one), in the name of maintaing the "plausible deniability" of US involvement, as to inalterably compromise any likelihood of its success. In October 1962, it was made public that the Soviets had clandestinely placed forty-two long-range missiles in Cuba, despite their assurances to the contrary. President Kennedy, responded by ordering a "quarantine" (a politically inspired term for assuaging the American public, as the majority of the missiles were already in Cuba). After days of tense negotiations the Soviets agreed to withdraw their missiles from Cuba in return for a secret American promise to dismantle similar missile sites from Turkey as well as in Northern Italy, and additionally promise not to invade the island to overthrow Castro's communist government. It took twenty-five years for the details of the blameworthy deal—long denied by Kennedy sycophants—to be fully and publicly acknowledged. On 22 November 1963, President Kennedy was assassinated by Lee Harvey Oswald while riding in a motorcade through Dallas, Texas. Hours later, Vice President Lyndon B. Johnson was inaugurated as president.

The "Great Society" Envisioned by Johnson

Lyndon B. Johnson overwhelmingly defeated his Republican opponent, Barry M. Goldwater, in the November 1964 elections, and embarked on his vision for a "Great Society"; a vigorous program of social legislation and deficit spending unsurpassed since Roosevelt's New Deal. His programs sought to ensure African-Americans' voting rights and increase public housing, provide persons age 65 and over with hospitalization and other medical benefits (i.e., the Medicare program), and provide job training to the poor and unemployod. the The woman's rights movement in the late 1960s also grew and paralleled measures ensuring equal opportunity for minority groups. The growth of a powerful environmental protection movement also occurred during this period (see Appendix 16: "The Great Society").

While Southeast Asia was still part of French Indochina, US military and economic aid to anti-Communist forces in Vietnam was begun during the Truman administration, and was gradually increased by Presidents Eisenhower and Kennedy. With the Gulf of Tonkin Resolution of 1964,

Congress gave President Lyndon B. Johnson authority to send US combat troops to prevent a communist takeover of South Vietnam. Additionally, President Johnson ordered US bombing raids over North Vietnam to halt their infiltration into the south and hamper their ability to wage war. By the fall of 1968, there were 536,100 American military personnel in Vietnam, but the US armed forces were unable to decisively defeat the Viet Cong (i.e., Vietnamese guerrillas), and American public opinion was divided over continuing the undeclared and perhaps ill-advised, war with its high cost in material and human casualties. Burdened with increasing dissatisfaction with his Vietnam policies, racial violence in major cities, and the assassination of Martin Luther KIng and Robert Kennedy, Johnson withdrew in March 1968 from the forthcoming presidential race, and in November seasoned Republican Richard M. Nixon, who had served as Vice President under Eisenhower, was elected President (see Appendix 17: "The Vietnam War"). Thus, the Johnson years—which had begun with the social engineering of the Great Society—soured and drew to a close.

[Image 14: President Lyndon B. Johnson greets American troops in Vietnam, 1966.]

President Nixon began the gradual withdrawal of US combat troops from Vietnam under the program of Vietnamization, while at the same time expanding aerial bombardment throughout Indochina to prompt the communists to the negotiation table and support the Army of the Republic of South Vietnam. The war continued in this manner for four more years before a cease-fire—negotiated by Nixon's consummate geopolitician and national security adviser, Henry Kissinger—was finally signed on 27

January 1973, and the last US combat troops were withdrawn. The longest war in American history had cost the US government $112 billion in military expenditures resulted in 46,163 US combat deaths and 303,654 wounded. Nixon intended ending the American combat role in Vietnam, but not necessarily abandoning the principle of containing communism in Southeast Asia. Campaigning to achieve "peace with honor" in Vietnam, Nixon promised that the United States would defend the South Vietnamese government should North Vietnam violate the peace accords. However, the North Vietnamese, who like other communist régimes operated under the premise of "what is mine, is mine, what is yours is negotiable" almost immediately began operations violating the peace accords. By December 1974, North Vietnamese forces invaded the South Vietnamese province of Phuoc Long. The communists sought to test the South Vietnamese and American response to the invasion.

As North Vietnamese forces advanced southward, President Gerald R. "Jerry" Ford requested a $522 million aid package for South Vietnam, but the American Congress, dominated by the Democrats, voted against the proposal, ignoring the communist violations and thus ensuring their victory. As the South Vietnamese government collapsed, 1,373 US citizens and 5,595 Vietnamese and third country nationals were evacuated from the South Vietnamese capital of Saigon during Operation Frequent Wind. North Vietnam's victory over the South led to a considerable loss of prestige for the US in Asia, as well as the enslavement of the South Vietnamese people by an inhumane communist dictatorship.

The Nixon-Kissinger Policy

On 20 July 1969, a major international triumph had been achieved by the United States by landing the first astronaut on the moon. Shortly after planting an American flag on the moon's surface, the two astronauts spoke to President Richard M. Nixon, who congratulated them on their mission. In 1972, at the peak of the Sino-Soviet split, Mao and Zhou Enlai met with President Nixon in Beijing to establish relations with the United States. A strategic arms limitation agreement was also signed with the Soviet Union, as part of the Nixon-Kissinger policy of pursuing détente with both major Communist powers. All were Nixonian modifications to the policy of containment. Yet, containment had not been abandoned, as evidenced by American covert assistance to Chilean opposition groups, leading to the overthrow of Salvador Allende's Marxist government in 1973. The Nixon administration sought to appeal to the "silent majority" of Americans in support of its Indochina policies, and in domestic affairs its conservative social outlook. One of the most momentous developments during President Nixon's administration was the Watergate scandal, which began with the arrest of five men associated with the President's reelection campaign on 17 June 1972, during a break-in at Democratic Party headquarters in the Watergate office building in Washington, DC. Although Nixon had been reelected in 1972, succeeding disclosures by investigative reporters and by a Senate committee revealed a series of duplicitous and illegal tactics of a political nature, and illegal domestic surveillance throughout his first term. The apparent attempts by the President to help his aides obstruct the investigation and judicial proceedings were confirmed by tape recordings of private conversations made by Nixon himself, which the Supreme Court ordered him to release for use as evidence in criminal proceedings. The House of Representatives, having a majority by the Democrats, voted to begin impeachment proceedings, and in late July 1974, its Judiciary Committee approved three articles of impeachment. In the name of national interest, on 9 August, Nixon became the first president to resign the office; although not impeached. During the following year, Nixon's former attorney general, John N. Mitchell, and some of his top aides were convicted of obstruction, and were subsequently sentenced to prison. In his resignation speech, the President stated,

"....I no longer have a strong enough political base in the Congress to....see the constitutional process through to its conclusion, that to do otherwise would be...a dangerously destabilizing precedent for the future....

I would have preferred to carry through to the finish whatever the personal agony it would have involved, and my family unanimously urged me to do so. But the interest of the Nation must always come before any personal considerations.

.... I have concluded that because of the Watergate matter I might not have the support of the Congress that I would consider necessary to back the very difficult decisions and carry out the duties of this office in the way the interests of the Nation would require."

Nixon's successor was his Nebraskan Vice President, Gerald R. Ford (1974–77); a consistent proponent of national defense, he led the Republican opposition to Johnson's Great Society programs and chairman of the Republican National Convention in 1968 and 1972.

In October 1973, Ford was appointed by President Nixon to succeed Vice President Spiro Agnew, who had resigned following his plea of *nolo contendere* to charges that he had failed to pay income tax on moneys he had received from contractors while governor of Maryland. As vice president, Ford traveled widely throughout the country to rally support for the Nixon administration, which had eroded as a result of the Watergate affair. His tenure as Vice President was short; when Nixon resigned, Ford became President. He pledged to continue Nixon's foreign policy and to work to curb inflation. One month later he issued a pardon to Nixon for any illegal acts that he may have committed while in office. In the 1974 congressional elections the Republicans suffered substantial losses, attributable both the economy and the Watergate affair. To deal with the economic recession, Ford proposed tax cuts, limited social spending, although maintaining high defense expenditures, and heavy taxation on imported oil. The Democratic Congress opposed many elements of the program. Ford was defeated by Democrat James E. "Jimmy" Carter Jimmy in the 1976 presidential election.

The Carter Years

With Carter's presidency, containment took a back seat to his concern for human rights abroad. Americans were at times confused and concerned about the direction of Carter's foreign policy: our diplomats had been taken hostage in Iran, and their rescue failed; he seemed unable to counter the Soviets' move into Afghanistan; the Castro-Cubans became involved in aiding pro-communist guerrillas and began sending troops throughout Africa; the Sandinistas had succeeded in Nicaragua, and the Cubans seemed to be doing as they pleased in the Americas.

Carter returned the Canal Zone to leftist dictator Omar Efraín Torrijos (who held titles including "Maximum Leader of the Panamanian Revolution"), a sycophant of Fidel Castro. Democrat and Republican opponents, including Ronald Reagan, actively campaigned against the Canal treaties, charging that the documents would surrender American territory which was essential to national security. To these people, the treaties seemed to symbolize American decline. Carter interpreted all this as a "malaise" infecting the American public, not a crisis of confidence resulting from his questionable leadership. Carter's anti-communist credentials were further tarnished by his administration's formalized relations with China in January 1979. He slashed defense spending drastically.

Early in his presidency, Jimmy Carter's was dovish and forbearing toward the Soviets. But as the Soviet tanks rolled into Afghanistan in December, 1979, the victimizable Carter was shocked into adopting a tougher foreign policy with regards to the USSR. The Carter administration provided limited covert aid to the anti-communist Mujehedeen forces in Afghanistan (a policy proposed by his national security adviser Zbigniew Brzezinski), cancelled grain shipments to the USSR, and boycotted the Olympics scheduled to be held in Moscow.

The Carter administration was not without a positive political legacy; it orchestrated the 1978 Camp David peace accords, the historic agreement forged between Anwar El-Sadat, the president of Egypt, and Menachem Begin, the new Israeli prime minister Israel, in Maryland. Under the agreement, Israel agreed to return the Sinai Peninsula to Egypt, and the two nations also agreed to negotiate measure for Palestinian autonomy. The peace agreement reoriented Egyptian foreign policy objectives; from an alliance with Moscow, to an alliance with Washington.

The continuing decline of the economy, high unemployment, and double-digit inflation caused his popularity to wane. The inability of his administration to obtain the release of more than 50 US hostages seized in Tehrān on 4 November 1979 contributed to increased public doubts about his leadership. The hostages were released on 20 January 1981, the day of Reagan's inauguration.

"Reaganomics", Revitalization, and Growth

A broad defense build-up began during the Reagan administration, as well as an increased the moral energy, purpose, and sense of urgency for countering the Soviets. Declaring in 1983 that the USSR was an "evil empire" which threatened world peace, President Ronald Wilson Reagan significantly changed the strategy of the Cold War and the policy of containment. Dubbed the "Reagan Doctrine", it was a sweeping and aggressive application of American political philosophy which challenged the fundamental legitimacy of all communist governments. It proclaimed the right, as well as the responsibility, of the United States to provide assistance to those movements seeking independence from communist régimes. In addition to giving greater military aid to the Mujehedeen in Afghanistan, including Stinger Missiles, the US provided military support to the anti-communist Angolan leader Jonas Savimbi's UNITA movement in Africa.

In Central America, Reagan provided covert aid to the "Contra" guerrillas attempting to overthrow the left-wing Sandinista government in Nicaragua, and sought to block efforts by the Sandinista-aided left-wing rebels to overthrow the US-supported government in El Salvador. In 1985, high-ranking Reagan administration officials sold arms clandestinely to Iran for its war against Iraq. The money from these arms sales was laundered in Israel and diverted to the anti-communist Contras in Nicaragua (i.e., the "Iran-Contra Affair": the disclosure prompted the resignation of two of the leaders of the group, Vice Admiral John Poindexter and Lieutenant Colonel Oliver North, as well as investigations by House and Senate committees and a special prosecutor, Lawrence Walsh. The congressional investigations found no conclusive evidence that Reagan had authorized or known of the diversion). In his last years in office, however, Reagan somewhat softened his anti-Soviet rhetoric as he worked on the Strategic Arms Reduction Talks—START. Many analysts argue that Reagan's policy of increased American military spending, especially in regards to the Strategic Defense Initiative (SDI, or "Star Wars") pressured the Soviets to increase their respective military spending, thus further exacerbating to their already severe economic problems and hastened their downfall.

[Image 15: US President Ronald Reagan (left) and Soviet General Secretary Mikhail Gorbachev (right) at the first Summit in Geneva, Switzerland. 19 November 1985.]

Having survived an assassination attempt in 1981, Reagan used his popularity to push through significant supply side economic policy changes, referred to as "Reaganomics". He succeeded in enacting income tax cuts of 25%, reducing the maximum tax rate on unearned income from 70% to 50%, and accelerating depreciation allowances for businesses. When he took office in January 1981 the American economy was suffering from slow growth, high inflation, rising unemployment, and unprecedented high interest rates. Yet, well before the end of his presidency in 1988, he had succeeded in reversing all of the problems he inherited, putting the American economy on the path of sound, noninflationary growth.

Widely praised and winning unanimous confirmation from the Senate, Reagan's appointment of Sandra Day O'Connor as the first woman justice of the Supreme Court was a historical first. He named Alexander M. Haig, Jr., former NATO supreme commander for Europe, to the post of secretary of state. Haig was replaced in 1982 by George P. Shultz.

George H.W. Bush

Reagan was succeeded in 1988 by his highly credentialed Vice President, George H.W. Bush. Due to the prolonged economic upswing created by Reagan's policies, Bush easily defeated liberal Democrat Michael Dukakis, governor of Massachusetts.

Containment—primarily as a policy seeking to stop Soviet/communist expansionism—was clearly no longer as relevant with the 1991 disintegration of the Soviet Union. The challenge to Bush and the following American presidents was to determine how much of the intrinsic anticommunism in the containment policy was relevant in dealing with the remaining and very different communist régimes in Cuba, North Korea, and China. Up through 2001, all US administrations remained hostile to Cuba, and unwilling to open relations with Fidel Castro's government. All American presidents continued to worry about North Korea, and instability on the Korean peninsula. For Presidents George H. W. Bush in 1989–1993 (and later Bill Clinton in 1993–2001, as well as the new George W. Bush presidency in 2001) the lure of trade with China, and frequently the belief that a softer rhetorical stance was better in improving human rights policies, would guide the uneasy and often shifting US policy toward China.

George H. W. Bush continued the Reagan Doctrine named after his predecessor, witnessed the final year of the Cold War, and the Gulf War against Saddam Hussein (see Appendix 18: "The Reagan Doctrine", and Appendix 19: "The Gulf War"). With the end of the Cold War, President Bush also received an economic "peace dividend" in the form of reduced defense expenditures. Prior to becoming president, Bush was appointed director of the CIA in 1976. He was credited with strengthening the intelligence community and helping to restore morale at the agency. In that office, Bush coordinated administration efforts to combat international terrorism and wage the international war on drugs, a portent of the changes that were to come after the fall of the USSR.

During the Bush presidency, relations between the brutal Panamanian dictator, Manuel Noriega, and the US were deteriorating beyond the point of repair. In October 1989, Noriega survived a coup by discontent Panamanian army officers, which was openly supported by the US. In the afterglow of his triumph, Noriega was boastful and vindictive, announcing that a state of undeclared war existed between Panama and the US. President Bush was concerned that Noriega would endanger the security of the canal, and further infuriated by the random firing on US soldiers by Panamanian Defense Forces. The murder of a US Marine in the streets of Panama City was the ultimate provocation, prompting Bush to authorize a full-scale invasion of that country (i.e., "Operation Just Cause") on 20 December 1989. After hiding in the Papal Nunciature, Noriega was captured, brought to the US for trial, and convicted in 1992 on charges of racketeering, money laundering, and drug trafficking. Noriega was sentenced to 40 years in prison and ordered to pay $ 44 million to the Panamanian government.

[Image 16: President George W. Bush (second from right) and his father, former President George H. W. Bush (third from right), look on as Italian Prime Minister

Silvio Berlusconi (right) and former President Bill Clinton (second from left) shake hands, 7 April 2005, prior to dinner at the Prime Minister's Rome residence. The visit came on the eve of the funeral for Pope John Paul II.]

After Iraqi dictator Saddam Hussein invaded Kuwait in August 1990, President Bush organized a 30-nation coalition of Western democracies, Japan, and some Arab states to liberate the tiny country dubbed "Operation Desert Storm". Launched on 17 January 1991, Desert Storm drove out the Iraqis in roughly a month of warcraft. The American people, grateful for the end of the "Vietnam syndrome" of defeatism, gave the president an 89 percent approval rating in the polls. As of this writing Operation Desert Storm stands as as the most exemplary feat of American international leadership, political resolve, and military effectiveness since World War II.

Another major Bush accomplishment in 1991 was the Strategic Arms Reduction Treaty (i.e., "START"), signed with Soviet leader Mikhail Gorbachev in July at their fourth summit conference, marking the end of the long nuclear arms race, as well as the first-ever agreement since the dawn of the atomic age in 1945 to dismantle and destroy nuclear weapons. After 40 years of Cold War tensions, unforeseen and monumentally historic changes became commonplace during George H. W. Bush's presidency: the unification of East and West Germany, the flowering of democracy in Eastern Europe and the Soviet Union, and the emergence of a new relationship with Russia. The totalitarian ideology of communism in Europe was indeed consigned to the ash heap of history.

Bush sought to maintain policies introduced by the Reagan administration on domestic issues. The establishment of strict regulations to limit air pollution, providing subsidies for child care, and protecting the rights of the disabled were some os his legislative initiatives.

During the late eighties, one of the biggest crises that the Bush administration encountered was the near collapse of the savings and loan industry (commonly referred to as the S&L crisis). The public generally perceived the economy as being weak during the election year, although data released indicated that a healthy rebound had already begun in 1992. Focusing on the financial concerns of what he called "the forgotten middle class," Democratic challenger Bill Clinton took advantage of this perception in his campaign.

Promising fiscal responsibility and economic growth, and taking a more centrist position on many issues than most liberal-leaning Democrats,

Clinton defeated Bush, winning 43% of the vote to Bush's 38%. Third-party candidate Ross Perot garnered 18% of the vote.

"Bill" Clinton

President George H. W. Bush's reelection campaign was weakened by his reversal on his 1988 promise not to raise taxes, the effects of the lingering 1990-1991 recession, dwindling public concerns over foreign policy dangers, and the third-party candidacy of Ross Perot, who divided the electorate into a three-way race.

With the cooperation of a Democratic Congress, in 1993 William J. Clinton signed into law the Family and Medical Leave Act, the Omnibus Budget Reconciliation Act, the Brady Handgun Violence Prevention Act, the AmeriCorps Act, and the North American Free Trade Agreement (NAFTA) in 1994.

The North American Free Trade Agreement

The NAFTA accord established a free-trade zone in North America between Canada, Mexico, and the United States. It lifted tariffs and called for the gradual elimination, over a period of 15 years, of barriers limiting the movement of goods, and of investment among the three countries. Major industries affected by the agreement include automobile, agriculture, textile manufacture, financial services, telecommunications, energy, trucking, labor and environmental cooperation. American union representatives claim the agreement has led to job loss in the United States, because industries have moved plants to Mexico (see Appendix 20: "NAFTA").

The most unsuccessful and controversial domestic policy initiative by Clinton was his proposed Health Security Act, a socialized health-care plan. Public and congressional opposition to the plan increased as its complex, confusing details became public. After the Republicans won control of Congress in 1994, Clinton reinvented himself as a centrist Democrat seeking bipartisan compromise and cooperation. Pressured by Republicans to practice fiscal responsibility, he signed the Welfare Reform Act of 1996 (which most House Democrats opposed). With no major foreign policy problems and a prosperous economy, Clinton was reelected in 1996.

Clinton engaged in brief, but unsuccessful military interventions in Haiti and Somalia. Together with NATO, the US engaged in aerial strikes to end "ethnic cleansing" in Serbia. When Iraqi dictator Saddam Hussein's expelled UN weapons inspectors and committed other violations of international law, Clinton publicly supported "régime change" in Iraq, but his military response was ineffectual and limited to launching cruise missiles.

The Clinton presidency was filled with scandal. Clinton experienced congressional, judicial, and media investigations due to the sexual harassment lawsuit filed against him by Paula Jones, Hillary Clinton's involvement in the failed Whitewater real estate investment corporation, and his firing of employees in the White House travel office. Perhaps the most damaging and notable scandal was his sexual affair with White House intern Monica Lewinsky, where at a January 1998 press conference, Clinton firmly denied having sexual relations with Lewinsky. The House of Representatives impeached Clinton on charges of perjury and obstruction of justice on 19 December 1998. After a trial in the Senate, then in the hands of Democrats, he was acquitted on 12 February, 1999.

As Clinton prepared to leave office in 2001, he attracted further controversy when pardoning Marc Rich, a billionaire who fled to Switzerland because of charges of tax evasion and violations of the oil embargoes against Iran and Libya. Rich's wife, Denise, had previously made substantial contributions to the Democratic Party and Clinton's presidential library and foundation.

By the year 2000 US demographics started to change; African Americans were replaced as the largest minority group by Hispanics, (Hispanics numbered 12.5 percent of the population, or 35.3 million inhabitants, compared with 34.7 million blacks, or 12.3% of the population.) The 2000 presidential election pitted Republican Party candidate George Walker Bush, son of former president George H. W. Bush, against Democratic vice president Al Gore. It became one of the closest political races in US history.

George W. Bush

Although the election was extremely close, and was finally resolved by a five to four decision of the U.S. Supreme Court, Bush emerged as the winner, capping a speedy rise to the nation's highest office in a relatively short political career that combined uncanny campaigning skills, good timing, and an influential family. Bush's victory represented the second time in American history that the son of a former president took on the world's most powerful political job.

Bush's governing style in Texas relied on bi-partisanship, and his ability to appeal both to the "old-guard" Republicans, who tended to be more moderate, and the Christian Right. Bush sewed up the GOP nomination by demonstrating his ability to attract millions in contributions, and establishing a jovial connection with a wide variety of people; his folksiness made Gore look stiff by comparison.

President Bush made education the top priority of his administration, signing the "no child should be left behind" Act, reauthorized the Elementary and Secondary Education Act, and supported standards-based education reform. He called for pay and benefit increases for the military, and enacted Medicare Part D (providing drug coverage) into law, and supported Social Security. He called upon faith based community groups and charities to provide aid the disadvantaged, and promoted pro-life policies like the Partial-Birth Abortion Ban Act. He implemented several free trade agreements and pushed for energy independence by promoting offshore and domestic oil drilling.

Bush also championed comprehensive immigration reform and Social Security reform, but the legislation for either cause never garnered enough support to overcome opposition in Congress by obstructionist Democrats. As economic stimulus designed to respond to an economy that had begun to falter, Bush implemented a $1.3 trillion tax cut plan in 2001 and 2003, significantly lowering the marginal tax rates for nearly all US taxpayers. He warned of the threat of international terrorism and called for research and development of a missile-defense program.

11 September 2001

The perils of international terrorism was made painfully obvious on 11 September 2001, when 19 hijackers crashed 4 passenger aircraft into the World Trade Center's North and South towers, the Pentagon, and a field in Pennsylvania's Stony Creek Township. Along with the destruction of the World Trade Center towers, approximately 3,000 people were killed as a result of all four 11 September 2001 attacks. Additionally 1,140 workers have been diagnosed with cancer caused by toxic smoke and particles from the collapse of the towers. Al-Qaeda, a Muslim terrorist organization led by Saudi-born Osama bin Laden, was identified as being responsible for the attacks, and a manhunt for bin Laden began.

On 7 October 2001, the US and UK launched air attacks against known military installations and terrorist training camps within Afghanistan, ruled by the Taliban régime that gave assistance to the al-Qaeda organization. The leaders of the European Union and Russia, as well as other nations, supported the air strikes. By December 2001, the Taliban régime had been defeated, and Afghan leader Hamid Karzai was chosen to lead an interim government. However, remnants of al-Qaeda fighters remained in Afghanistan and the surrounding regions, and by 2013 up to 60,000 US military personnel remained in Afghanistan to suppress efforts by al-Qaeda or the Taliban to regroup.

[Image 17: President George W. Bush greets and offers words of hope and consolation to rescue workers at the site of the collapsed World Trade Center. New York, NY, 14 September 2001.]

As a response to the increased needs for national security after the 11 September 2001 terrorist attacks, President Bush signed the USA PATRIOT Act enhancing law enforcement investigatory tools related to terrorism, and established the Department of Homeland Security. The act expanded the powers of the federal government and local law enforcement to detain suspected terrorists, to counter money-laundering, and increase surveillance. Critics of the Patriot Act maintain that the law does not conform to the system of checks and balances that safeguard civil liberties in the United States.

Beginning in late 2001, the energy giant Enron Corporation declared bankruptcy after false accounting practices were made public. In 2002 telecommunications giant WorldCom also revealed massive financial mismanagement, which led to its bankruptcy; one of the largest in US history.

In his January 2002 State of the Union Address, President Bush condemned Iran, Iraq, and North Korea as part of an "axis of evil," which violated human rights, sponsored terrorism, and sought weapons of mass destruction (WMDs). The US pressed its case against Iraq throughout 2002, stating that Saddam Hussein's régime had to disarm itself of weapons of mass destruction. The UN Security Council passed Resolution 1441 in November 2002, calling upon Iraq to disarm itself of any chemical, biological, or nuclear weapons and to allow for the immediate return of weapons inspectors, which had been expelled since 1998. Weapons inspectors from the UN and IAEA (International Atomic Energy Agency) returned to Iraq, but their progress was greatly obstructed by the Iraqi government, and President Bush indicated that military force might be necessary to remove the noncompliant régime of Saddam Hussein. Disagreement on whether to use military force caused a diplomatic rift in the West, as France and Russia, permanent members of the UN Security Council, and Germany, a nonpermanent member, opposed such action.

Iraqi Freedom

After diplomatic efforts to continue the inspections unhampered failed, on 19 March, the war began as the US launched air strikes against Iraqi targets. Iraq's armed forces proved to be no match, and on 9 April, Baghdad fell to US forces. Immediately work began on restoring safe drinking water, electricity, sanitation, and other basic services to the Iraqi population. On 1 May, President Bush declared major combat operations had been completed. On 13 December 2003 Iraq's former dictator, Saddam Hussein, was captured by US forces and placed in custody to await trial (see Appendix 21: "The Iraq War").

In May 2004, the Abu Ghraib scandal flared. Photographs of US soldiers engaged in acts of abuse against Iraqi prisoners being held at the Abu Ghraib military prison outside Baghdad were publicized. The US Department of Defense removed seventeen soldiers and officers from duty, and eleven soldiers were charged with maltreatment, aggravated assault and battery, and dereliction of duty. Brigadier General Janis Karpinski, the commanding officer of all Iraq detention facilities, was reprimanded for dereliction of duty and demoted to the rank of Colonel on May 2005. Col. Karpinski denied knowledge of the abuses, claiming that the interrogations were authorized by her superiors and performed by subcontractors.

To counter a persistent insurgency, in January 2007, President Bush presented a new strategy based on the strategies and tactics developed by General David Petraeus. A troop surge in 2007 was part of this "new way forward" and, along with a change in tactics and US alliances with Sunni groups, has been credited with an 80 percent decrease in violence. On 1 September 2010, the US officially ended combat operations, and the last American troops exited Iraq on 18 December 2011.

In the 2004 presidential election President George W. Bush and Vice President Dick Cheney easily defeated Democratic challengers John F. Kerry and John R. Edwards. Bush received approximately 3 million more popular votes than Kerry, and won the electoral vote 286 to 251. Issues as terrorism, the War in Iraq, the economy, and to a lesser extent issues of morality and values—were all favorable to the Bush/Cheney ticket.

Hurricane Katrina

In what was to become one of the worst natural disasters in US history, Hurricane Katrina made landfall on the Gulf Coast of the United States in August 2005. The low-lying city of New Orleans, Louisiana, was partially evacuated, but some 150,000 people were unable to leave. The storm surge breached the protective levees and water submerged major portions of the city.

President Bush sent the resources of the Federal Emergency Management Agency (FEMA) to the South in the wake of the hurricane, but soon came under intense criticism that the federal government had not done enough to aid the affected population. New Orleans Mayor Ray Nagin was also criticized for delaying the evacuation, and ordering residents to shelters of last resort; the Louisiana Superdome and New Orleans Convention Center. There, air conditioning, electricity, and running water failed, making for unsanitary and uncomfortable conditions without food, water, or security. The Mayor also refused to use idle school buses to evacuate, on the grounds that it would raise liability issues. Nagin's decisions directly led to hundreds of deaths of people who could not find any way out of the city.

FEMA director Michael D. Brown later resigned his position amid the furor. Race and class issues also came to the fore, as the majority of New Orleans residents unable to evacuate the city and were affected by the catastrophe were poor and African American. This was a particularly unwarranted charge since Mayor Ray Nagin is an African American (on 18 January 2013, Nagin was indicted on 21 corruption charges, including bribery, wire fraud, and money laundering related to his alleged dealings with city vendors following Hurricane Katrina disaster). The victims were later transferred to the Houston Astrodome and other shelters. Looting, shootings, and carjackings exacerbated already devastating conditions. The costs of the hurricane and flooding were extremely high: at least 1,800 people deaths and an estimated at $81 billion (in 2005 US dollars) in property damages.

In the final months of his administration, Bush presided over the beginnings of a recession in 2008, and set in motion several economic initiatives to preventing a banking system collapse, stopping bank foreclosures of homes, and stimulating the economy. In the international arena, President Bush signed the US-India Civil Nuclear Agreement, greatly improving relations between the two countries, and established an AIDS program that committed $15 billion to combat the disease over five years, especially in Africa; the President's Emergency Plan for AIDS Relief (PEPFAR). Perhaps his greatest legacy was that there were no successful terrorist attacks on the United States homeland after 11 September 2001.

[Image 18: The Presidents of the United States of America. Left to right former President George H.W. Bush, then President-Elect Barack Obama, President

George W. Bush, former President Bill Clinton, and former President Jimmy Carter at a Meeting and Lunch at The White House. Photo taken Wednesday, 7 Jan. 2009 in the Oval Office at the White House.]

SOURCES

America's Century: Year by Year from 1900–2000. London: Dorling Kindersley, 2000.

AP Students (2013). AP United States History: About the Exam. The College Board. Retrieved 25 November 2013 from https://apstudent.collegeboard.org/apcourse/ap-united-states-history/about-the-exam.

Benjamin, Daniel (ed.) (2005). *America and the World in the Age of Terror: A New Landscape in International Relations*. Washington, D.C.: CSIS Press.

Céspedes, Juan R. (2012). *20th century history and contemporary issues class lecture notes*. Unpublished documents. Florida International University, Miami, Florida.

Céspedes, Juan R. (2012). *IB History Exam Study Guide: International Contemporary History 1848-2008*. CreateSpace.

Chambers, S. Allen. *National Landmarks, America's Treasures: the National Park Foundation's Complete Guide to National Historic Landmarks*. New York: J. Wiley and Sons, 2000.

Davies, Philip John. (ed.) *An American Quarter Century: US Politics from Vietnam to Clinton*. New York: Manchester University Press, 1995.

Davis, Tom (2005, 15 September). Select Bipartisan Committee to Investigate the Preparation for and Response to Hurricane Katrina. A Failure of Initiative;
The Final Report of the Select Bipartisan Committee to Investigate the Preparation for and Response to Hurricane Katrina. Retrieved 22 December 2013 from http://www.katrina.house.gov.

Donaldson, Gary. *America at War since 1945: Politics and Diplomacy in Korea, Vietnam, and the Gulf War*. Westport, Conn.: Praeger, 1996.

Encyclopedia of the Nations (2013). United States - History. Advameg. Retrieved 24 December 2013 from http://www.nationsencyclopedia.com/Americas/United-States-HISTORY.html#b.

Frontline, PBS (2005, 22 November posting). The Storm. Retrieved 22 December 2013 from http://www.pbs.org/wgbh/pages/frontline/storm/view/.

Hart, James David (ed.). *Oxford Companion to American Literature*. 6th ed. New York: Oxford University Press, 1995.

Health in the Americas, 2002 edition. Washington, D.C.: Pan American Health Organization, Pan American Sanitary Bureau, Regional Office of the World Health Organization, 2002.

Hummel, Jeffrey Rogers. *Emancipating Slaves, Enslaving Free Men: A History of the Civil War*. Chicago: Open Court, 1996.

Jenness, David. *Classic American Popular Song: The Second Half-Century, 1950–2000*. New York: Routledge, 2006.

Kaplan, Edward S. *American Trade Policy, 1923–1995*. Westport, Conn.: Praeger, 1996.

Kennedy, David M. *Freedom from Fear: The American People in Depression and War*. New York: Oxford University Press, 2001.

Marston, Daniel (2002). *The American War of Independence: 1774–1783*. London, UK: Osprey.

McElrath, Karen (ed.). *HIV and AIDS: A Global View*. Westport, Conn.: Greenwood Press, 2002.

McNickle, D'Arcy. *Native American Tribalism: Indian Survivals and Renewals*. New York: Oxford University Press, 1993.

Newell, Clayton R. *United States Army, a Historical Dictionary*. Lanham, Md.: Scarecrow Press, 2002.

PBS. Presidential Links. Nixon's Resignation Speech Auguat 8, 1974. Retrieved 13 December 2013 from *http://www.pbs.org/newshour/character/ links/nixon_speech.html*.

Rein, Meiling, Nancy R. Jacobs, Maek S. Siegel (eds.). *Immigration and Illegal Aliens: Burden or Blessing?* Wylie, Tex.: Information Plus, 1999.

Robinson, Cedric J. *Black Movements in America*. New York: Routledge, 1997.

Sampanis, Maria. *Preserving Power through Coalitions: Comparing the Grand Strategy of Great Britain and the United States*. Westport, Conn.: Praeger, 2003.

Sinclair, Andrew. *A Concise History of the United States*. Rev. ed. Stroud: Sutton, 1999.

Sullivan, Meg (2004, 10 August). FDR's policies prolonged Depression by 7 years, UCLA economists calculate. UCLA Newsroom. Retrieved 25 December 2013 from http://newsroom.ucla.edu/portal/ucla/fdr-s-policies-prolonged-depression-5409.aspx

Summers, Randal W., and Allan M. Hoffman (ed.). *Domestic Violence: A Global View*. Westport, Conn.: Greenwood Press, 2002.

Tocqueville, Alexis de. *Democracy in America*. New York: Knopf, 1994.

"United States." Worldmark Encyclopedia of Nations. 2007. Retrieved September 22, 2013 from Encyclopedia.com: http://www.encyclopedia.com/doc/1G2-2586700176.html.

US Bureau of the Census. *Historical Statistics of the United States, Colonial Times to 1970*. Washington, D.C.: US Government Printing Office, 1879-date.

Utley, Jon (2000, 8 February) MOST-HATED SENATOR WAS RIGHT. *Scholars: Joseph McCarthy's charges 'now accepted as fact'. WND (World Net Daily). Retrieved 25 December 2013 from* http://www.wnd.com/2000/02/4020/.

York, Neil (2003). *Turning the World Upside Down: The War of American Independence and the Problem of Empire*. New York: Praeger.

IMAGES

Front cover: Washington Crossing the Delaware (cropped close up). Artist: Emanuel Leutze, 1851. Oil on Canvas. Metropolitan Museum of Art. Source photographer: Web Gallery of Art. This is a faithful photographic reproduction of a two-dimensional work of art. Such reproductions are in the public domain in the United States and those countries with a copyright term of life of the author plus 100 years or less.

Back cover: "The Bennington Battle Flag" flying outside City Hall in San Francisco, California. 11 October 2008. Author: Makaristos. Released to the public domain.

Image 1: Christopher Columbus, painting by Sebastiano del Piombo (1519). Current location: Metropolitan Museum of Art. This work is in the public domain in the United States, and those countries with a copyright term of life of the author plus 100 years or less.

Image 2: Image 2: Colonial kitchen with woman spinning, an engraving. 1885. Source: A Brief History of the United States by Joel Dorman Steele and Esther Baker Steele, 1885. This image is in the public domain because its copyright has expired.

Image 3: The Second Continental Congress voting independence. Author unknown. U.S. Constitution Sesquicentennial Commission. (1935 - ca. 12/31/1939). National Archives and Records Administration. Still Pictures Records Sections. Identifier #532839. This work is in the public domain in the United States under the terms of Title 17, Chapter 1, Section 105 of the US Code.

Image 4: The "Committee of Five" that drafted the U.S. Declaration of Independence. Composite of paintings of various authors. Left to right: Roger Sherman, painting by Ralph Earl (1751–1801), 1775-1776; Benjamin Franklin, painting by Jean-Baptiste Greuze (1725–1805), 1777; Thomas Jefferson, painting by Charles Willson Peale (1741–1827), 1791; John Adams, painting by Asher Brown Durand (1796–1886); Robert R. Livingston, painting by Charles Wilson Peale (1741-1827, 1781/82). These are faithful photographic reproductions of a two-dimensional, public domain works of art. Such reproductions are in the public domain in the United States because their copyright has expired.

Image 5: Portrait of Thomas Jefferson by Rembrandt Peale, 1800. Source: White House Historical Association. This work is in the public domain in the United States, and those countries with a copyright term of life of the author plus 100 years or less.

Image 6: A covered wagon at the Texas Parks and Wildlife Expo 2007. Date: 7 October 2007. Source/author: © 2007 Larry D. Moore, photographer (CC BY-SA 3.0). This image is licensed under the Creative Commons Attribution-Share Alike 3.0 Unported license.

Image 7: Abolitionist John Brown, 1854. Source: The Magazine of American History with Notes and Queries ed.), A.S. Barnes, 1893, OCLC 1590082, http://openlibrary.org/books/OL20455410M/ The_Magazine_of_American_History_with_Notes_and_Queries. Unattributed authorship. This media file is in the public domain of the United States because the copyright has expired, and the publication occurred prior to 1 January 1923.

Image 8: Abraham Lincoln, Republican candidate for the presidency, 1860. Created/Published: New York : Published by W. Schaus, 629 Broadway, c1860 (Boston : Printed at J.H. Bufford's). This image is available from the United States Library of Congress's Prints and Photographs division under the digital ID cph.3c23259. Lithographer: Grozelier, Leopold (1830-1865). Painter: Hicks, Thomas, 1823-1890. This work is in the public domain in the United States, and those countries with a copyright term of life of the author plus 100 years or less.

Image 9: Smartly dressed couple seated on an 1886-model bicycle for two. The South Portico of the White House, Washington, DC, in the background. Author unknown. Record creator: War Department. Office of the Chief of Engineers. (1818 - 09/18/1947). Current location of image: National Archives and Records Administrations, College Park, Still Picture Records Section, Special Media Archives Services Division (NWCS-S). Cataloged under the ARC Identifier (National Archives Identifier) 519711. The National Archives and Records Administration provides images depicting American and global history which are public domain or licensed under a free license.

Image 10: A Renault Tank model WWI. Author unknown. Source: The Brigade http://thebrigade.thechive.com/2013/02/10/trench-war-in-the-1917-18-renault-ft-17-tank-52-photos/. Retrieved 27 December 2013. Author unknown. This image is in the public domain in the United States because its copyright has expired.

Image 11: Mlle. Rhea seated with flask in garter on leg. Photograph made on 26 January 1926, during prohibition in the United States. This file comes from the Historic American Buildings Survey (HABS), Historic American Engineering Record (HAER) or Historic American Landscapes Survey (HALS). These are programs of the National Park Service established for the purpose of documenting historic places. Records consist of measured drawings, archival photographs, and written reports. This work is in the public domain in the United States because it is a work prepared by an officer or employee of the United States Government as part of that person's official duties under the terms of Title 17, Chapter 1, Section 105 of the US Code.

Image 12: The Great Depression. Breadlines:long line of people waiting to be fed: New York City: in the absence of substantial government relief programs during 1932, free food was distributed with private funds in some urban centers to large numbers of the unemployed. Author unknown. Circa February 1932. Current location: National Archives and Records

Administration. Identifier # 196506. Series: Franklin D. Roosevelt Library Public Domain Photographs, compiled 1882 - 1962.

Image 13: An SBD Dauntless dropping its bomb. The SBD ("Scout Bomber Douglas") was the U.S. Navy's main carrier-borne scout plane and dive bomber from mid-1940 through mid-1944. Source http://www.nasascale.org/museum_pensacola.htm. This file is a work of a sailor or employee of the U.S. Navy, taken or made as part of that person's official duties. As a work of the U.S. federal government, the image is in the public domain.

Image 14: President Lyndon B. Johnson greets American troops in Vietnam, 1966. Author: U.S. Information Agency. This work was obtained from the now defunct United States Information Agency. In 1999 the agency was merged into the Bureau of Public Affairs which is the part of the United States Department of State. This work is in the public domain in the United States because it is a work of the United States Federal Government under the terms of 17 U.S.C. § 105.

Image 15: US President Ronald Reagan (left) and Soviet General Secretary Mikhail Gorbachev (right) at the first Summit in Geneva, Switzerland. 19 November 1985. Ronald Reagan Presidential Library photo id C31982-11. Author unknown. This image is a work of an employee of the Executive Office of the President of the United States, taken or made as part of that person's official duties. As a work of the U.S. federal government, the image is in the public domain.

Image 16: President George W. Bush (second from right) and his father, former President George H. W. Bush (third from right), look on as Italian Prime Minister Silvio Berlusconi (right) and former President Bill Clinton (second from left) shake hands, 7 April 2005, prior to dinner at the Prime Minister's Rome residence. The visit came on the eve of the funeral for Pope John Paul II. White House photo by Eric Draper. This image is a work of an employee of the Executive Office of the President of the United States, taken or made as part of that person's official duties. As a work of the U.S. federal government, the image is in the public domain.

Image 17: President Bush greets and offers words of hope and consolation to rescue workers at the site of the collapsed World Trade Center. New York, NY, 14 September 2001 -- Photo by SFC Thomas R. Roberts/ NGB-PASE. This image is a work of a Federal Emergency Management Agency employee, taken or made as part of that person's official duties. As works of the U.S. federal government, all FEMA images are in the public domain.

Additional media usage information may be found at http://www.fema.gov/ help/usage.shtm.

Image 18: The Presidents of the United States of America. Left to right former President George H.W. Bush, then President-Elect Barack Obama, President George W. Bush, former President Bill Clinton, and former President Jimmy Carter at a Meeting and Lunch at The White House. Photo taken Wednesday, 7 Jan. 2009 in the Oval Office at the White House. Source: http://georgewbush-whitehouse.archives.gov/news/ releases/2009/01/images/20090107-3_ky2q3150-515h.html. Author: Joyce N. Boghosian. This image is a work of an employee of the Executive Office of the President of the United States, taken or made as part of that person's official duties. As a work of the U.S. federal government, the image is in the public domain.

APPENDICES

APPENDIX 1: "FRENCH AND INDIAN WARS"

[Excerpts from "French and Indian Wars." Columbia Encyclopedia. 2013. Retrieved 26 December, 2013 from Encyclopedia.com: http://www.encyclopedia.com/topic/ French_and_Indian_Wars.aspx#2]

[The] French and Indian Wars, 1689–1763, [was] the name given by American historians to the North American colonial wars between Great Britain and France in the late 17th and the 18th cent. They were really campaigns in the worldwide struggle for empire and were roughly linked to wars of the European coalitions. At the time they were viewed in Europe as only an unimportant aspect of the struggle, and, although the stakes were Canada, the American West, and the West Indies, the fortunes of war in Europe had more effect in determining the winner than the fighting in the disputed territory itself.

To the settlers in America, however, the rivalry of the two powers was of immediate concern, for the fighting meant not only raids by the French or the British but also the horrors of tribal border warfare. The conflict may be looked on, from the American viewpoint, as a single war with interruptions. The ultimate aim—domination of the eastern part of the continent—was the same; and the methods—capture of the seaboard strongholds and the little Western forts and attacks on frontier settlements—were the same.

The wars helped to bring about important changes in the British colonies. In addition to the fact of their ocean-wide distance from the mother country, the colonies felt themselves less dependent militarily on the British by the end of the wars; they became most concerned with their own problems and put greater value on their own institutions. In other words, they began to think of themselves as American rather than British....

APPENDIX 2: "AMERICAN REVOLUTIONARY WAR"

[Excerpts from "War of Independence." West's Encyclopedia of American Law. 2005. Retrieved 24 September 2013 from Encyclopedia.com: http:// www.encyclopedia.com/doc/1G2-3437704643.html]

The War of Independence, also known as the American Revolution and the Revolutionary War, was fought from 1775 to 1783 between Great Britain and the 13 British colonies in North America. The 1783 treaty of Paris, which ended the war, gave the 13 colonies political independence and led to the formation of the United States of America.

The war had its roots in the...limited political freedom granted by Great Britain to the colonists for managing their affairs. Acts of British Parliament in the 1760s that imposed taxes and import duties on the colonies increased these tensions.

The British victory in the French and Indian War, also known as the Seven Years' War (1756–63), removed France as a power in North America, yet the costs of the war were staggering for Great Britain. Faced with a large national debt, Parliament passed the Molasses Act and the Sugar Act in 1764, which imposed a duty on molasses and sugar imported by the colonies. The stamp act of 1765 taxed papers such as legal documents, newspapers, and almanacs. The Quartering Act indirectly taxed the colonists by requiring them to house, feed, and supply British troops.

American colonists reacted angrily to these tax measures, believing that it was unfair of Great Britain to subject them to taxation when the colonies had no representation in Parliament. British leaders repealed the Stamp Act in 1766, but the following year Parliament passed the Townshend act, which imposed a series of new taxes on goods arriving at American ports. The new taxes were designed to pay the salaries of royal governors and other colonial appointees of Britain's King George III. The Townshend Act also restructured the customs service in the colonies, placing its headquarters in Boston.

The Townshend Act evoked more protests from the colonists. Groups such as the Sons of Liberty and the Daughters of Liberty organized protests against customs officials and boycotts of taxed goods. Merchants agreed not to sell imported goods.

British customs agents in Boston extorted money and seized American ships with little justification, leading to a riot in March 1770. The British troops, popularly known as redcoats because of their red uniforms, fired on the crowd, killing five people. The episode became known as the boston massacre.

Great Britain again reacted to economic pressure by removing most of the Townshend Act taxes. A notable exception was the tax on tea, which remained a symbol of Parliament's authority to tax colonists. In 1773 Britain tried to save the financially troubled British East India Company by passing the Tea Act, which lowered the tax on tea shipped by the company to the colonies, giving the company an edge over tea smugglers. The colonists responded by refusing to buy English tea and refusing to allow it to be unloaded from British ships. In Boston protesters dressed as American Indians dumped crates of tea into the water, and the event came to be known as the Boston Tea Party.

Parliament retaliated in 1774 by passing the Coercive Acts, which were labeled the "Intolerable Acts" by the colonists. These laws closed the port of Boston until the East India Company was repaid for the dumped tea, restricted the powers of the Massachusetts colonial legislature, and permitted British soldiers and officials accused of capital crimes to be tried in England rather than in the hostile colony. In addition, Parliament appointed General Thomas Gage, commander of the British Army in North America, as the governor of Massachusetts. Gage was to enforce the Coercive Acts.

Representatives of 12 colonies and Canada met in September 1774 to consider what action to take against Parliament. The delegates to the First continental congress agreed that the colonies, and not Parliament, had the right to tax and make laws for the colonies. They called for a complete trade boycott against Britain until the Coercive Acts were repealed, but they acknowledged Parliament's right to regulate trade. The Congress did not call for independence from Great Britain.

The war began in 1775 when General Gage tried to break up a Massachusetts militia group and seize its ammunition and supplies. On the evening of April 18, 1775, Gage ordered his troops to seize munitions at Concord. Militia messengers, including silversmith Paul Revere, rode on horseback the 18 miles from Boston to Concord to warn the militia. Militia forces met the redcoats in Lexington, and they exchanged fire. The British killed eight men and proceeded to Concord, where they again encountered militia companies. The British retreated to Boston after 273 redcoats were killed in the battle. The militia followed, laying siege to the city for almost one year.

In early May 1775 colonial delegates met in Philadelphia for the Second Continental Congress. The New England militia was renamed the Continental Army, and george washington, a Virginia plantation owner who had served in the French and Indian War, was named commander. The delegates also made the Congress the central government for "The United Colonies of America."

King George III replaced Gage with General William Howe. The king had become concerned over mounting British casualties that accompanied battles in Massachusetts, including the Battle of Bunker Hill. On August 23, 1775, the king declared the colonies to be in rebellion and subjected colonial ships to seizure.

American troops invaded Canada in August 1775, capturing Montreal in November. However, their efforts to take the city of Quebec failed, and the troops were forced to withdraw. During the winter of 1775–76, Washington positioned artillery around Boston. In March 1776 a massive artillery attack on the city led British troops and more than one thousand Loyalists (colonists who supported the British) to flee on ships to Nova Scotia, Canada.

In June 1776, as the British assembled reinforcements for an invasion, the Continental Congress debated a declaration of the colonies' independence from Britain. thomas jefferson borrowed from the recently completed virginia declaration of rights in drafting the Declaration of Independence. The Virginia declaration, written by george mason, stated that government derived from the people, that individuals were created equally free and independent, and that they had inalienable rights that the government could not legitimately deny them. On July 4, 1776, the Congress declared that the colonies were free and independent states, and it adopted the Declaration of Independence.

On June 29, 1776, Howe led an invasion force of 32,000 troops, including 18,000 German mercenaries (Hessian troops), that landed off Sandy Hook, New Jersey. The British attacked Washington's forces in New York on August 22, and by the end of the year Washington had abandoned New York City and had moved his troops into Pennsylvania. He made a successful surprise attack on Trenton, New Jersey, on December 25, 1776. On January 3, 1777, Washington's troops defeated the British at Princeton, New Jersey. The two victories were critical to maintaining colonial morale, and by the spring of 1777 more than 8000 new soldiers had joined the Continental Army.

The British implemented a plan in 1777 that sought to end the war that year by separating New England from the colonies in the south. General John Burgoyne led British forces from Montreal toward Albany, New York. After securing a victory at Fort Ticonderoga on July 5, Burgoyne became overconfident. The Continental Army and local militia counterattacked, forcing Burgoyne to surrender his army after a battle at Saratoga, New York, on October 17.

To the south, Washington vainly tried to stop the British from taking Philadelphia, the home of the Continental Congress. His troops lost at the battle of Brandywine Creek, and Philadelphia fell to the British on September 26. The Congress moved to Baltimore, Maryland.

Despite the loss of Philadelphia and some discontent with Washington's leadership during the winter of 1777–78, American fortunes brightened in 1778. In February France signed a formal treaty of commerce and alliance with the American states. France sent a naval fleet along with military advisers and financial aid.

In June 1778 Washington attacked the British at Monmouth, New Jersey, but again was defeated. He then shifted his military strategy, keeping his troops encamped around British forces in Connecticut, New York, and New Jersey. Although American forces led by George Rogers Clark regained control of the Ohio River Valley, British troops had success in South Carolina in 1779. However, in 1780 American troops prevailed in the Battle of Kings Mountain and again in the Battle of Cowpens in 1781. The British attempt to control the southern colonies ended in a stalemate.

In 1781 Washington's troops, with the assistance of the French Navy, cut off British forces led by General Charles Cornwallis at Yorktown, Virginia. The Battle of Yorktown, in which British troops were outnumbered two to one, ended in a British surrender on October 19, 1781. This marked the end of major military actions in the War of Independence.

The defeat at Yorktown led to the resignation of the British prime minister and a desire by the new cabinet to begin peace negotiations, which commenced in Paris, France, in April 1782. The U.S. delegation included benjamin franklin, john adams, and john jay. The negotiators concluded a preliminary treaty on November 30, 1782, and a final agreement was signed in September 1783 and ratified by the Continental Congress on January 14, 1784.

In the Treaty of Paris the British recognized the independence of the United States. The treaty established generous boundaries for the United

States, with U.S. territory extending from the Atlantic Ocean to the Mississippi River in the west, and from the Great Lakes and Canada in the north to the thirty-first parallel in the south. The U.S. fishing fleet was guaranteed access to the fisheries off the coast of Newfoundland, Canada. Navigation of the Mississippi River was to be open to both the United States and Great Britain....

APPENDIX 3: "JEFFERSONIAN PRINCIPLES"

[Excerpts, from Vance, Laurence M. (2004, 1 September). Jeffersonian Principles. LewRockwell.com. Retrieved 28 November 2013 from http:// archive.lewrockwell.com/vance/vance17.html]

Peace is our most important interest, and a recovery from debt.

The happiness of mankind is best promoted by the useful pursuits of peace.

Agriculture, manufactures, commerce and navigation, the four pillars of our prosperity, are the most thriving when left most free to individual enterprise.

War is not the best engine for us to resort to, nature has given us one in our commerce, which, if properly managed, will be a better instrument for obliging the interested nations of Europe to treat us with justice.

This quote is part of Jefferson's annunciation of what he deemed "the essential principles of our government." The quote in its context reads as follows:

About to enter, fellow citizens, on the exercise of duties which comprehend everything dear and valuable to you, it is proper that you should understand what I deem the essential principles of our government, and consequently those which ought to shape its administration. I will compress them within the narrowest compass they will bear, stating the general principle, but not all its limitations. Equal and exact justice to all men, of whatever state or persuasion, religious or political; peace, commerce, and honest friendship with all nations — entangling alliances with none; the support of the State governments in all their rights, as the most competent administrations for our domestic concerns and the surest bulwarks against anti-republican tendencies; the preservation of the general government in its whole constitutional vigor, as the sheet anchor of our peace at home and safety abroad; a jealous care of the right of election by the people — a mild and safe corrective of abuses which are lopped by the sword of the revolution where peaceable remedies are unprovided; absolute acquiescence in the decisions of the majority — the vital principle of republics, from which there is no appeal but to force, the vital principle and immediate parent of despotism; a well-disciplined militia — our best reliance in peace and for the first moments of war, till regulars may relieve them; the supremacy of the civil over the military authority; economy in the public expense, that labor may be lightly burdened; the honest payment of our debts and sacred preservation of the public faith; encouragement of agriculture, and of commerce as its handmaid; the diffusion of information and the arraignment of all abuses at the bar of public reason; freedom of religion; freedom of the press; freedom of person under the protection of the habeas corpus; and trail by juries impartially selected — these principles form the bright constellation which has gone before us, and guided our steps through an age of revolution and reformation.

APPENDIX 4: "WAR OF 1812"

[Excerpts from Lerner, Adrienne Wilmoth. "War of 1812." Encyclopedia of Espionage, Intelligence, and Security. 2004. Retrieved 24 September 2013 from Encyclopedia.com: http://www.encyclopedia.com/doc/1G2-3403300807.html]

The War of 1812, spawned by the European Napoleonic Wars, was the last war in which the fledgling United States fought its former colonial power, Great Britain. After three years of fighting on land and at sea, the United States military successfully drove the British forces from United States soil, but not before British troops burned Washington, D.C. The War of 1812 assured the United States the independent sovereignty it claimed after victory in the American Revolution and shaped American foreign policy for over a century.

When continental Europe erupted in conflict in 1793, the United States declared itself neutral...the United States tried to remain out of contentious European politics, especially in regards to European colonial holdings in the Americas. Relations were further strained by British resentment of ongoing United States trade and diplomatic cooperation with France. British ships blockaded United States ports, hoping to prevent supplies and trade goods from reaching France. United States leaders, George Washington and John Adams, worked to ease tensions and lift the blockade, and by 1795, the nation again conducted trade with allies in Europe. However, by 1803, the United States government grew deeply concerned about the presence of a strong British military force in the Great Lakes region. Negotiations with Britain to reduce their military presence in the West and along the northern border of New England failed. Tensions again mounted when France sold the United States significant territories, including the Mississippi River, in the Louisiana Purchase.

In 1805, the British Navy resumed its blockade of the Unites States coast, prohibiting the export of most goods to continental Europe. The Orders in Council of 1807 further restricted neutral trade with Europe, and authorized British ships to take both the cargo and crew of seized neutral ships. The practice of impressment, forcing captured seamen into service on British ships, inflamed anti-British sentiment in the United States. The passage of the Embargo Act, confining all United States trade to the North American coast, the failure of continued diplomatic relations, and British-incited Indian attacks on United States outposts, gave credence to the opinions of the "War Hawks" in the United States government. In June 1812, the United States declared war on Britain.

The War of 1812 forced the United States to rapidly form and train military forces. After the Revolutionary War, the federal government only reluctantly allowed provisions for national forces. Most armies were maintained by individual states, with little standardization of training and equipment. The war spanned the entire breadth of the United States and its territories, from the Great Lakes region to New Orleans, Louisiana. Regional armies facilitated troop movement and deployment, but the lack of national infrastructure made travel and communication among the different battlefronts difficult. Military generals attempted to create a complex communication and espionage network, utilizing couriers on horseback and semaphore, to deliver messages. Codes were primitive and easy to break, but both British and American forces employed invisible inks to help conceal communications.

The vast expanses of rough and unfamiliar territory that both armies traversed required the extensive use of scouts. Both British and American forces preferred to use Indian scouts, who often had superior knowledge of regional terrain and could communicated in several indigenous languages. Indian scouts also aided in the recruitment of Indians to fight rival forces. British and United States military leaders also attempted to spark warfare between rival tribes with varying allegiances, hoping to distract opposing forces or break their aid network. Extensive contact with indigenous populations proved devastating, as during the American Revolution, disease ravaged Indian villages and several thousand Indian warriors died in battle.

From 1812 to 1814, the United States suffered numerous crushing defeats at the hands of superior British forces. United States offensives failed to take the Great Lakes region, and military defenses could not keep British troops from occupying Washington, D.C. Anticipated French aid never materialized in the 1813, as the tide of war in Europe had shifted decisively in favor of the British, and Napoleon's French Empire was in grave danger of collapse. American diplomats in Paris maintained a small espionage network in Europe and the Americas to monitor the British military and diplomatic corps. A French spy, posing as a local trader, rode to the White House to inform the president and cabinet members of the British plans to invade, occupy, and then destroy Washington, D.C. The government fled the British invasion of the capital city, but only by a matter of hours.

Despite the grim prospects of the United States land campaign in the early years of the war, the new United States Navy mounted surprisingly successful battles against the powerful British Navy. The United States reluctantly formed its Navy to combat the extortionist trade monopoly of the North African Barbary Pirates who dominated shipping in the

Mediterranean. While wealthier European government simply paid annual tributes and occasional ransoms to the Barbary authorities, the fledgling United States Federal government could not afford to pay such large sums of money. The nation mounted a small but highly effective Navy, eventually driving the Barbary authorities to capitulation. After the conflict, the government only narrowly voted to keep naval forces.

When the British began the blockade of the American coastline, United States navy and merchant ships successfully ran the blockade. The government employed "pirate" ships to destroy British ships, and recapture seized cargo and Americans impressed into service. With the outbreak of war, naval resources were increasingly devoted to strategic sea campaigns against British vessels. The United States Navy successfully captured the British frigate *Macedonian*, defeated the *Java*, and raided several other merchant and military ships. Victories at sea, though limited, enforced the need for a permanent navy in the United States and ensured its continued survival. One hundred and forty years later, the United States Navy surpassed the British fleet to become the world's dominant sea power.

As the French were defeated in Europe, the British devoted more resources to the battlefront in America. However, United States forces rallied, turning the tide of the war in their favor by August 1814. Wishing to avoid clear military defeat, both sides began peace negotiations. The British failure to capture Baltimore prompted the government to settle their dispute with the United States, instead of continuing a lingering, expensive, and increasingly stalemated overseas war. The Treaty of Ghent formally ended the war in 1815. On January 8, 1815, after the signing of the treaty, United States forces, commanded by Andrew Jackson, achieved a stunning victory against the British at the port of New Orleans. Since communication was tedious across the Atlantic and the expansive western territory of Louisiana, news of the Treaty of Ghent did not reach either forces in time to prevent the engagement. The Battle of New Orleans gave the impression that the long-stalemated war was a sound United States victory, but the new nation was successful largely because of the failure of British offensive operations.

After the War of 1812, the United States declared firmer international policy. With the issuance of the Monroe Doctrine in 1823, the nation stated its policy of non-intervention in European conflicts. Furthermore, the United States declared the New World closed to further colonization, and that attempts of foreign powers to intervene in conflicts between colonial powers and their colonies would be viewed as an act of aggression. The War of 1812 solidified the political and military preeminence of the United

States in the Americas, and began the great expansion westward toward the Pacific coast.

APPENDIX 5: "MONROE DOCTRINE"

[Excerpts from Whiteclay Chambers II, John. "Monroe Doctrine." The Oxford Companion to American Military History. 2000. Retrieved 24 September 2013 from Encyclopedia.com: http://www.encyclopedia.com/doc/1O126-MonroeDoctrine.html]

In his message of 2 December 1823, President James Monroe articulated two principles that by the 1850s were regarded as the basis for the so-called Monroe Doctrine. The first stipulated that the "American Continents, by the free and independent condition which they have assumed and maintain, are henceforth not to be considered as subjects for future colonization by any European Power." The second embodied Monroe's support for the newly independent Latin American republics by stating that the American and European political systems were "essentially different," and that the United States would consider efforts by European nations "to extend their system to any portion of this hemisphere as dangerous to our peace and safety."

James K. Polk, in the 1840s, was the first president to invoke Monroe's message as a form of policy justification... For much of the nineteenth century the Monroe Doctrine was ignored or violated far more than it was observed. U.S. acquiescence in such developments as the British occupation of the Falkland Islands (1833), British activities in the Central American isthmus throughout the 1850s, Spain's reannexation of Santo Domingo in 1861, and France's installation of a Bourbon monarch in Mexico in the 1860s were hardly in accord with the principles of 1823.

In the last quarter of the nineteenth century, in response to rising concerns about European imperialism coupled with a more assertive sense of American nationalism, the United States began to invoke the Monroe Doctrine more consistently. This was particularly so in 1895, when the Cleveland administration insisted, successfully, that Great Britain submit to arbitration a long-standing boundary dispute between Venezuela and British Guiana. On that occasion Secretary of State Richard Olney formulated the first major corollary to the 1823 message by asserting that "the United States is practically sovereign on this continent, and its fiat is law upon the subjects to which it confines its interposition."

After the turn of the century, the United States redefined the Monroe Doctrine in ways that were also intended to justify greater U.S. activity in the Americas. In 1904, President Theodore Roosevelt, anxious that financial malfeasance in the nations of Central America and the Caribbean might provoke intervention by European creditor nations, announced a second major corollary to the Monroe Doctrine to the effect that no

American nation could use the doctrine "as a shield to protect it from the consequences of its own misdeeds against foreign nations." In effect, this required the United States to intervene in the affairs of other American nations. Acting on this basis, the United States took over the management of the finances of the Dominican Republic (in 1907) and of Nicaragua (in 1911), and in 1915 it actually occupied the republic of Haiti.

The assumptions behind the "Roosevelt corollary," although repudiated in the 1930s in favor of Franklin D. Roosevelt's "Good Neighbor" policy, continued to influence U.S. policy in the Americas through the 1980s. Beginning with Woodrow Wilson, U.S. presidents have sought to reconcile the regional principles of the doctrine with the increasingly global reach of their foreign policies. Worried about aggression from Nazi Germany, Franklin Roosevelt even expanded the doctrine to include both Canada and Greenland.

In the early years of the Cold War after 1945, the United States internationalized the democratic and noninterventionist principles of the Monroe Doctrine in the Truman Doctrine of 1947, while at the same time it preserved its regional hegemony in the Americas through the framework of the Rio Pact (1947) and the Organization of American States (1948). The concern to keep communism out of the Americas subsequently led to U.S. intervention in various forms in Guatemala (1954), Cuba (1961), the Dominican Republic (1965), Chile (1973), and Grenada (1983), as well as to active involvement in the insurgencies in El Salvador and Nicaragua in the 1980s. In each case the United States either overthrew, or attempted to overthrow, left-wing regimes in order to replace them with dictatorial governments whose members supported U.S. priorities. Critics argued that these repressive governments violated the principles that Monroe had proclaimed in 1823.

The most serious crisis of the Monroe Doctrine occurred in Communist Cuba in 1962. As early as 1960, Soviet premier Nikita Khrushchev openly proclaimed that the Monroe Doctrine was dead. Two years later, Khrushchev installed intermediate-range missiles on the island to protect Fidel Castro's regime. Throughout the ensuing Cuban Missile Crisis, which was eventually resolved by the removal of the missiles, President John F. Kennedy did not invoke the Monroe Doctrine in defense of his actions, but concern for its traditions was never far from his mind.

With the end of the Cold War in 1991 and the disappearance of any regional threats to the security of the United States in the western hemisphere, the Monroe Doctrine might be fairly regarded as moribund, if not entirely dead. The doctrine was never accepted as valid international law by any European nation, and it would be inaccurate to say that it saved Latin America from any form of recolonization. Nor did the doctrine ever receive much support in Latin America; indeed, to the extent that the United States invoked it in the twentieth century, it became increasingly unpopular there as a symbol of an overbearing Yankee supremacy. The true significance of the Monroe Doctrine, however, has always depended on circumstances.

APPENDIX 6: "MEXICAN-AMERICAN WAR"

[Excerpts from "Mexican-American War." Dictionary of American History. 2003. Retrieved 24 September 2013 from Encyclopedia.com: http:// www.encyclopedia.com/doc/1G2-3401802626.html]

Mexican-American War(1846–1848). The war's remote causes included diplomatic indiscretions during the first decade of American-Mexican relations, as well as the effects of the Mexican revolutions, during which American citizens suffered physical injury and property losses. Its more immediate cause was the annexation of Texas. The Mexican government refused to recognize Texas as independent or the Rio Grande as an international boundary....

President James K. Polk anticipated military action and sent Brigadier General Zachary Taylor with his force from Louisiana to the Nueces River in Texas, but he also sought a diplomatic solution. Recognizing that the chief aim of American foreign policy was the annexation of California, Polk planned to connect with that policy the adjustment of all difficulties with Mexico, including the dispute over jurisdiction in the territory between the Nueces River and the Rio Grande.

In September 1845, assured through a confidential agent that the new Mexican government of José Joaquín Herrera would welcome an American minister, and acting on the suggestion of Secretary of State James Buchanan, Polk appointed John Slidell as envoy-minister on a secret mission to secure California and New Mexico for $15 million to $20 million if possible, or for $40 million if necessary—terms later changed by secret instructions to $5 million for New Mexico and $25 million for California.

Mexico refused to reopen diplomatic relations. In January 1846, after the first news that the Mexican government, under various pretexts, had refused to receive Slidell, partly on the ground that questions of boundary and claims should be separated, Polk ordered Taylor to advance from Corpus Christi, Texas, to the Rio Grande, resulting shortly in conflicts with Mexican troops at the battle of Palo Alto on 8 May and the battle of Resaca de la Palma on 9 May. On 11 May, after arrival of news of the Mexican advance across the Rio Grande and the skirmish with Taylor's troops, Polk submitted to Congress a war message stating that war existed and that it was begun by Mexico on American soil. The United States declared war on 13 May, apparently on the ground that such action was justified by the delinquencies, obstinacy, and hostilities of the Mexican government; and Polk proceeded to formulate plans for military and naval operations to advance his goal of obtaining Mexican acceptance of his overtures for peace negotiations.

The military plans included an expedition under Colonel Stephen W. Kearny to New Mexico and from there to California, supplemented by an expedition to Chihuahua; an advance across the Rio Grande into Mexico by troops under Taylor to occupy the neighboring provinces; and a possible later campaign of invasion of the Mexican interior from Veracruz.

In these plans Polk was largely influenced by assurances received in February from Colonel A. J. Atocha, a friend of Antonio López de Santa Anna, then in exile from Mexico, to the effect that the latter, if aided in plans to return from Havana, Cuba, to Mexico, would recover his Mexican leadership and cooperate in a peaceful arrangement to cede Mexican territory to the United States. In June, Polk entered into negotiations with Santa Anna through a brother of Slidell, receiving verification of Atocha's assurances. Polk had already sent a confidential order to Commodore David Conner, who on 16 August permitted Santa Anna to pass through the coast blockade to Veracruz. Having arrived in Mexico, Santa Anna promptly began his program, which resulted in his own quick restoration to power. He gave no evidences whatever of his professed pacific intentions.

On 3 July 1846 the small expedition under Kearny received orders to go via the Santa Fe Trail from Fort Leavenworth, Kansas, to occupy New Mexico. It reached Santa Fe on 18 August, and a part of the force (300 men) led by Kearny marched to the Pacific at San Diego. From there it arrived at Los Angeles to join the forces led by Commodore Robert Field Stockton, including John Charles Frémont's Bear Flag insurgents. Kearny and Stockton joined forces and defeated the Mexican army at Los Angeles on 8 and 9 January 1847. On 13 January, Frémont and Andres Pico, the leader of the Mexican forces in California, signed the Treaty of Cahuenga. Kearny went on to establish a civil government in California on 1 March.

Taylor's forces, meanwhile, began to cross the Rio Grande to Matamoros on 18 May 1846 and advanced to the strongly fortified city of Monterrey, which after an attack was evacuated by Mexican forces on 28 September. Later, in February 1847 at Buena Vista, Taylor stubbornly resisted and defeated the attack of Santa Anna's Mexican relief expedition.

Soon thereafter the theater of war shifted to Veracruz, from which the direct route to the Mexican capital seemed to present less difficulty than the northern route. In deciding on the campaign from Veracruz to Mexico City, Polk probably was influenced by the news of U.S. occupation of California, which reached him on 1 September 1846. The U.S. Navy had helped secure Monterrey, San Diego, and San Francisco in California and had continued blockades against Veracruz and Tampico. The Navy provided valuable assistance again when General Winfield Scott began a siege of Veracruz. After the capture of the fortress of Veracruz on 29 March 1847, Scott led the army westward via Jalapa to Pueblo, which he entered on 15 May and from which he began his advance to the mountain pass of Cerro Gordo on 7 August.

Coincident with Scott's operations against Veracruz, Polk began new peace negotiations with Mexico through a "profoundly secret mission." On 15 April, Buchanan had sent Nicholas P. Trist as a confidential peace agent to accompany Scott's army. In August, after the battles of Contreras and Churubusco, Trist arranged an armistice through Scott as a preliminary step for a diplomatic conference to discuss peace terms—a conference that began

on 27 August and closed on 7 September by Mexican rejection of the terms offered. Scott promptly resumed his advance. After hard fighting from 7 to 11 September at the battles of Molino del Rey and Chapultepec, he captured Mexico City on 14 September and with his staff entered the palace, over which he hoisted the American flag.

Practically, the war was ended. Santa Anna, after resigning his presidential office, made an unsuccessful attempt to strike at the American garrison Scott had left at Pueblo, but he was driven off and obliged to flee from Mexico.

The chief remaining American problem was to find a government with enough power to negotiate a peace treaty to prevent the danger of American annexation of all Mexico. Fortunately, Trist was still with the army and in close touch with the situation at the captured capital. Although recalled, he determined to assume the responsibility of remaining to renew efforts to conclude a peace treaty even at the risk of disavowal by his government. After some delay, he was able to conclude with the Mexican commissioners a treaty in accord with the instructions that had been annulled by his recall. The chief negotiations were conducted at Mexico City, but the treaty was completed and signed on 2 February 1848 at the neighboring town of Guadalupe Hidalgo. By its terms, which provided for cessation of hostilities, the United States agreed to pay $15 million for New Mexico and California. Polk received the treaty on 19 February and promptly decided to submit it to the Senate, which approved it on 10 March by a vote of thirty-eight to fourteen. Ratifications were exchanged on 30 May 1848.

Among the chief results of the war were expansion of American territory; a new population called Mexican Americans; increased American interest in the problems of the Caribbean and the Pacific and in the opening and control of isthmian interoceanic transit routes at Panama, Nicaragua, and Tehuantepec; and outbursts of "manifest destiny" from 1848 to 1860. The acquisition of Mexico's northern lands also intensified debates over the extension of slavery into new territory and brought the Union a step closer to war.

APPENDIX 7: "CIVIL WAR"

[Excerpts from "Civil War (in U.S. history)." The Columbia Encyclopedia, 6th ed.. 2013. Retrieved 24 September 2013 from Encyclopedia.com: http:// www.encyclopedia.com/doc/1E1-CivilWarUS.html]

Civil War, in U.S. history, conflict (1861–65) between the Northern states (the Union) and the Southern states that seceded from the Union and formed the Confederacy. It is generally known in the South as the War between the States...., the War of Secession, and the War for Southern Independence. The name Civil War, although much criticized as inexact, is most widely accepted.

Causes

The name Civil War is misleading because the war was not a class struggle, but a sectional combat having its roots in political, economic, social, and psychological elements so complex that historians still do not agree on its basic causes. It has been characterized, in the words of William H. Seward, as the "irrepressible conflict." In another judgment the Civil War was viewed as criminally stupid, an unnecessary bloodletting brought on by arrogant extremists and blundering politicians. Both views accept the fact that in 1861 there existed a situation that, rightly or wrongly, had come to be regarded as insoluble by peaceful means.

In the days of the American Revolution and of the adoption of the Constitution, differences between North and South were dwarfed by their common interest in establishing a new nation. But sectionalism steadily grew stronger. During the 19th cent. the South remained almost completely agricultural, with an economy and a social order largely founded on slavery and the plantation system. These mutually dependent institutions produced the staples, especially cotton, from which the South derived its wealth. The North had its own great agricultural resources, was always more advanced commercially, and was also expanding industrially.

Hostility between the two sections grew perceptibly after 1820, the year of the Missouri Compromise, which was intended as a permanent solution to the issue in which that hostility was most clearly expressed—the question of the extension or prohibition of slavery in the federal territories of the West. Difficulties over the tariff (which led John C. Calhoun and South Carolina to nullification and to an extreme states' rights stand) and troubles over internal improvements were also involved, but the territorial issue nearly always loomed largest. In the North moral indignation increased with the rise of the abolitionists in the 1830s. Since slavery was unadaptable to much of the territorial lands, which eventually would be admitted as free states, the South became more anxious about maintaining its position as an equal in the Union. Southerners thus strongly supported the annexation of Texas (certain to be a slave state) and the Mexican War and even agitated for the annexation of Cuba.

The Compromise of 1850 marked the end of the period that might be called the era of compromise. The deaths in 1852 of Henry Clay and Daniel Webster left no leader of national stature, but only sectional spokesmen, such as W. H. Seward, Charles Sumner, and Salmon P. Chase in the North and Jefferson Davis and Robert Toombs in the South. With the Kansas-Nebraska Act (1854) and the consequent struggle over "bleeding" Kansas the factions first resorted to shooting. The South was ever alert to protect its "peculiar institution," even though many Southerners recognized slavery as an anachronism in a supposedly enlightened age. Passions aroused by arguments over the fugitive slave laws (which culminated in the Dred Scott Case) and over slavery in general were further excited by the activities of the Northern abolitionist John Brown and by the vigorous proslavery utterances of William L. Yancey, one of the leading Southern fire-eaters.

The Election of 1860

The "wedges of separation" caused by slavery split large Protestant sects into Northern and Southern branches and dissolved the Whig party. Most Southern Whigs joined the Democratic party, one of the few remaining, if shaky, nationwide institutions. The new Republican party, heir to the Free-Soil party and to the Liberty party, was a strictly Northern phenomenon. The crucial point was reached in the presidential election of 1860, in which the Republican candidate, Abraham Lincoln, defeated three opponents— Stephen A. Douglas (Northern Democrat), John C. Breckinridge (Southern Democrat), and John Bell of the Constitutional Union party.

Lincoln's victory was the signal for the secession of South Carolina (Dec. 20, 1860), and that state was followed out of the Union by six other states —Mississippi, Florida, Alabama, Georgia, Louisiana, and Texas. Immediately the question of federal property in these states became important, especially the forts in the harbor of Charleston, S.C. (see Fort Sumter). The outgoing President, James Buchanan, a Northern Democrat who was either truckling to the Southern, proslavery wing of his party or sincerely attempting to avert war, pursued a vacillating course. At any rate the question of the forts was still unsettled when Lincoln was inaugurated, and meanwhile there had been several futile efforts to reunite the sections, notably the Crittenden Compromise offered by Sen. J. J. Crittenden.

Lincoln resolved to hold Sumter. The new Confederate government under President Jefferson Davis and South Carolina were equally determined to oust the Federals.

Sumter to Gettysburg

When, on Apr. 12, 1861, the Confederate commander P. G. T. Beauregard, acting on instructions, ordered the firing on Fort Sumter, hostilities officially began. Lincoln immediately called for troops to be used against the seven seceding states, which were soon joined by Arkansas, North Carolina, Virginia, and Tennessee, completing the 11-state Confederacy. In the first important military campaign of the war untrained Union troops under Irvin McDowell, advancing on Richmond, now the Confederate capital, were routed by equally inexperienced Confederate soldiers led by Beauregard and Joseph E. Johnston in the first battle of Bull Run (July 21, 1861). This fiasco led Lincoln to bring up George B. McClellan (1826–85), fresh from his successes in W Virginia (admitted as the new state of West Virginia in 1863).

After the retirement of Winfield Scott in Nov., 1861, McClellan was for a few months the chief Northern commander. The able organizer of the Army of the Potomac, he nevertheless failed in the Peninsular campaign (Apr.–July, 1862), in which Robert E. Lee succeeded the wounded Johnston as commander of the Confederate Army of Northern Virginia. Lee planned the diversion in the Shenandoah Valley, which, brilliantly executed by Thomas J. (Stonewall) Jackson, worked perfectly. Next to Lee himself Jackson, with his famous "foot cavalry," was the South's greatest general.

Lee then went on to save Richmond in the Seven Days battles (June 26–July 2) and was victorious in the second battle of Bull Run (Aug. 29–30), thoroughly trouncing John Pope. However, he also failed in his first invasion of enemy territory. In September, McClellan, whom Lincoln had restored to command of the defenses of Washington, checked Lee in Maryland (see Antietam campaign). When McClellan failed to attack the Confederates as they retreated, Lincoln removed him again, this time permanently.

Two subsequent Union advances on Richmond, the first led by Ambrose E. Burnside (see Fredericksburg, battle of) and the second by Joseph Hooker (see Chancellorsville, battle of), ended in resounding defeats (Dec. 13, 1862, and May 2–4, 1863). Although Lee lost Jackson at Chancellorsville, the victory prompted him to try another invasion of the North. With his lieutenants Richard S. Ewell, James Longstreet, A. P. Hill, and J. E. B. (Jeb) Stuart, he moved via the Shenandoah Valley into S Pennsylvania.

There the Army of the Potomac, under still another new chief, George G. Meade, rallied to stop him again in the greatest battle (July 1–3, 1863) of the war (see Gettysburg campaign).

Naval Engagements

With the vastly superior sea power built up by Secretary of the Navy Gideon Welles, the Union established a blockade of the Southern coast, which, though by no means completely effective, nevertheless limited the South's foreign trade to the uncertain prospects of blockade-running. In cooperation with the army the Union navy also attacked along the coasts. The forts guarding New Orleans, the largest Confederate port, fell (Apr. 28, 1862) to a fleet under David G. Farragut, and the city was occupied by troops commanded by Benjamin F. Butler (1818–93). The introduction of the ironclad warship (see Monitor and Merrimack) had revolutionized naval warfare, to the ultimate advantage of the industrial North. On the other hand, Confederate cruisers, built or bought in England (see Alabama claims) and captained by men such as Raphael Semmes, destroyed or chased from the seas much of the U.S. merchant marine.

The War in the West

That the "war was won in the West" has become axiomatic. There the rivers, conveniently flowing either north (the Cumberland and the Tennessee) or south (the Mississippi), invited Union penetration, as they did not in Virginia. In Feb., 1862, the Union gunboats of Andrew H. Foote forced the Confederates to retire from their post Fort Henry on the Tennessee to their stronghold on the Cumberland, Fort Donelson. There, on Feb. 16, 1862, Grant, commanding the Army of the Tennessee, won the first great Union victory of the war, and Nashville promptly fell without a struggle.

Farther down the Tennessee, Grant was lucky to escape defeat in a bloody contest (Apr. 6–7) with Albert S. Johnston and Beauregard (see Shiloh, battle of). Minor Union successes at Iuka (Sept. 19) and Corinth (Oct. 3–4) followed, while the counterinvasion by the Confederate Army of Tennessee under Braxton Bragg was stopped by Don Carlos Buell at Perryville, Ky. (Oct. 8, 1862). William S. Rosecrans, Buell's successor, then stalked Bragg through Tennessee, fought him to a standoff at Murfreesboro (Dec. 21, 1862–Jan. 2, 1863), and finally, by outmaneuvering him, forced the Confederate general to withdraw S of Chattanooga.

Union gunboats had cleared the upper Mississippi (see Island No. 10; Fort Pillow), leading to the fall of Memphis on June 6, 1862. Grant's Vicksburg campaign, at first stalled by the raids of Confederate cavalrymen Nathan B. Forrest and Earl Van Dorn, was pressed to a victorious end in a brilliant movement in which the navy, represented by David D. Porter, also had a hand. The Union now controlled the whole Mississippi, and the trans-Mississippi West was severed from the rest of the Confederacy. The fighting in that area (see Pea Ridge; Arkansas Post) had held Missouri for the Union and led to the partial conquest of Arkansas, but after the fall of Vicksburg, the war there, with the exception of the unsuccessful Union Red River expedition of Nathaniel P. Banks and a last desperate Confederate raid into Missouri by Sterling Price (both in 1864), was largely confined to guerrilla activity.

The Emancipation Proclamation

Britain never formally recognized the Confederacy (neither did France) and maintained peaceful relations with the Union despite the provocation late in 1861 of the Trent Affair, which was adroitly handled by Secretary of State Seward. Charles Francis Adams (1807–86) at London and John Bigelow at Paris were able diplomats, but probably more important in winning popular support for the Union in England and France was the Emancipation Proclamation, which Lincoln issued after Antietam.

This act appeased for a time the anti-Lincoln radical Republicans in Congress, among them Benjamin F. Wade, Zachariah Chandler, Thaddeus Stevens, and Henry W. Davis, with whom Secretary of the Treasury Salmon P. Chase and Secretary of War Edwin M. Stanton were allied. Not all Unionists were abolitionists, however, and the Emancipation Proclamation was not applied to the border slave states: Delaware, Maryland, Kentucky, and Missouri had all remained loyal. For Lincoln and kindred moderates, such as Postmaster General Montgomery Blair, the restoration of the Union, not the abolition of slavery, remained the principal objective of the war.

Turning Point

The Union victories at Gettysburg and Vicksburg in July, 1863, marked a definite turning point in the war. Both sides now had seasoned, equally valiant soldiers, and in Lee and Ulysses S. Grant each had a superior general. But the North, with its larger population and comparatively enormous industry, enjoyed a tremendous material advantage. Both sides also resorted to conscription, even though it met some resistance (see draft riots).

Under Stanton, successor to Simon Cameron, the overall administration of the Union army was more efficient. Problems of organization still remained, however, and Henry W. Halleck continued in the difficult role of military adviser, with the title of general in chief. The Joint Congressional Committee on the Conduct of the War, organized in Dec., 1861, attempted to influence the actions as well as the appointment of Union generals (its efforts were particularly strong on behalf of Hooker). The chairman, Benjamin F. Wade, was frequently at odds with Lincoln, and the committee's investigations and high-handed actions lowered morale among the Union forces.

Grant and Sherman

On the Georgia-Tennessee line in Sept., 1863, Bragg, having temporarily halted his retreat, severely jolted the Federals, who were saved from a complete rout by the magnificent stand of George H. Thomas, the Rock of Chickamauga (see Chattanooga campaign). Grant, newly appointed supreme commander in the West, hurried to the scene and, with William T. Sherman, Hooker, and Thomas's fearless troops, drove Bragg back to Georgia (Nov. 25). After Knoxville, occupied in September, withstood Longstreet's siege (Nov.–Dec.), all Tennessee, hotbed of Unionism, was now safely restored to the Union.

In Mar., 1864, Lincoln, for many years an admirer of Grant, made him commander in chief. Leaving the West in Sherman's capable hands, Grant came east, took personal charge of Meade's Army of the Potomac, and engaged Lee in the Wilderness campaign (May–June, 1864). Outnumbered but still spirited, the Army of Northern Virginia was slowly and painfully forced back toward Richmond, and in July the tenacious Grant began the long siege of Petersburg.

Although Jubal A. Early won at Monocacy (July 9), threatening the city of Washington, the Confederates were unable to repeat Jackson's successful diversion of 1862, and Philip H. Sheridan, victorious in the grand manner at Cedar Creek (Oct. 19), virtually ended Early's activities in the Shenandoah Valley. For his part, Sherman, opposed first by the wily Joe Johnston and then by John B. Hood, won the Atlanta campaign (May–Sept., 1864).

The Election of 1864

On the political front, a movement within the Republican party to shelve Lincoln had collapsed as the tide turned in the Union's favor. With Andrew Johnson, Lincolm's own choice for Vice President over the incumbent Hannibal Hamlin, the President was renominated in June, 1864. The Democrats nominated McClellan, who still had a strong popular following, on an ambiguous peace platform (largely dictated by Clement L. Vallandigham, leader of the Copperheads), which the ex-general repudiated. Even so, Lincoln was easily reelected.

Lee's Surrender

After the fall of Atlanta, which had contributed to Lincoln's victory, Sherman's troops made their destructive march through Georgia. Hood had failed to draw Sherman back by invading Union-held Tennessee, and after the battle of Franklin (Nov. 30) Hood's army was almost completely annihilated by Thomas at Nashville (Dec. 15–16, 1864). Sherman presented Lincoln with the Christmas gift of Savannah, Ga., and then moved north through the Carolinas. Farragut's victory at Mobile Bay (Aug. 5, 1864) had effectively closed that port, and on Jan. 15, 1865, Wilmington, N.C., was also cut off (see Fort Fisher).

After Sheridan's victory at Five Forks (Apr. 1), the Petersburg lines were breached and the Confederates evacuated Richmond (Apr. 3). With his retreat blocked by Sheridan, Lee, wisely giving up the futile contest, surrendered to Grant at Appomattox Courthouse (see under Appomattox) on Apr. 9, 1865. The surviving Confederate armies also yielded when they heard of Lee's capitulation, thus ending the conflict that resulted in some 620,000 casualties (with more recent estimates suggesting the number could be 750,000 or more).

Aftermath

The long war was over, but for the victors the peace was marred by the assassination of Abraham Lincoln, the greatest figure of the war. The ex-Confederate states, after enduring the unsuccessful attempts of Reconstruction to impose a new society on the South, were readmitted to the Union, which had been saved and in which slavery was now abolished. The Civil War brought death to more Americans than did any other war, including World War II. Photographs by Mathew B. Brady and others reveal some of the horror behind the statistics. The war cost untold billions and nourished rather than canceled hatreds and intolerance, which persisted for decades. It established many of the patterns, especially a strong central government, that are now taken for granted in American national life. Virtually every battlefield, with its graves, is either a national or a state park. Monuments commemorating Civil War figures and events are conspicuous in almost all sizable Northern towns and are even more numerous in the upper South.

APPENDIX 8: "RECONSTRUCTION"

[Excerpts from Whiteclay Chambers II, John. "Reconstruction." The Oxford
Companion to American Military History. 2000. Encyclopedia.com. Retrieved 26
December 2013 from http://www.encyclopedia.com/topic/Reconstruction.aspx#3]

...When the Confederate forces surrendered in April 1865, the U.S. Army
embarked on a mission unparalleled in its history: the postwar occupation
of a rebellious section of its own country as the enforcer of a politically
determined process of reconstruction. No previous war had required such
duty. During the Civil War, reconstruction had begun haltingly in 1862 in
those parts of Louisiana, Tennessee, Arkansas, and Virginia under Union
military control. However, Abraham Lincoln's "ten percent" plan for the
restoration of individual loyalty and government functions was at best
experimental. Military efforts remained focused on victory rather than postwar expectations.

Confederate surrender changed the picture entirely. Many parts of the
South had by now experienced the presence of Union troops. Neither
soldiers nor civilians knew how long that presence might last, nor what
policies would govern the relationship between victor and vanquished. The
Constitution, not having anticipated a breakup of the Union by force, gave
little specific guidance for the aftermath of such an effort. Federal statutes
were equally uninformative on the peacetime use of military power in
support of federal political processes. The American tradition of civil control
of military institutions was well developed, yet that tradition would not
provide clear answers to the many specific questions of power soon to
arise. Other complicating factors were the clamor of volunteer troops to go
home as soon as possible; the legislative need to establish a peacetime
size for the regular army; the resumption of patrol and Indian-fighting
duties in the West; and the need for troops to support diplomatic moves
against the French presence in Mexico.

During the twelve years of Reconstruction (1865–77), the army's
experience in the South evolved significantly as its powers, functions, and
problems changed. Five distinct phases can be identified. An initial period
of six weeks extended from mid–April 1865 to the end of May. The
Confederate national government had collapsed and in many states there
were no civil governments functioning. Legislators, governors, judges,
aldermen, sheriffs, and other local officials were not at their posts. Thus the
army, by default, assumed the task of local government.

Applying to civil government its familiar pattern of military administration,
the army established departments, districts, and subdistricts throughout the

South. Commanding officers of troops doubled as executive officers of government, or sought to find loyal and trustworthy civilians whom they could temporarily appoint to vacant positions. Considerations of workload as well as personal ability led army officers to prefer a pattern of civilian officeholders working under military orders.

The broad category of regulation called the police power, focusing on the health, safety, welfare, and morals of the community, came under military supervision. Specific subjects varied widely depending on local conditions. Typical regulations applied to collection of garbage, disinfecting alleys and streets with lime, naked children in public, dogs running at large, public profanity, speed limits for carriages, whitewashing of tree trunks, vagrancy, prostitution, distribution of food relief, and reopening of schools. Some commanders required proof of having taken the loyalty oath as a qualification for certain services, including receipt of mail or obtaining a marriage license. Approximately 250,000 troops remained in the South in the weeks immediately following the surrender. They performed a wide variety of different duties without adequate training. Commanding generals, some of whom were not regulars, often had to act on their own judgment or a highly general letter of instruction from superiors. The war had ended with a military surrender, not a treaty of peace, and the future policy of the government was initially unsettled.

On 29 May 1865, President Andrew Johnson issued two proclamations that would begin a period of "presidential Reconstruction." One prescribed a loyalty oath, established the terms of a general amnesty, and specified a process whereby those excluded from the general amnesty could apply for individual pardon. The second appointed a provisional governor for North Carolina and set forth a process for the reestablishment of a permanent state government and election of local officials. Thus began the second phase of the army's role in the South, which would extend until December 1865. Johnson shortly issued proclamations establishing provisional governments in South Carolina, Georgia, Florida, Alabama, Mississippi, and Texas. In Tennessee, Arkansas, Louisiana, and Virginia, the provisional governments established during the war continued.

The army's presence in the South now had a specific focus. The provisional governors were to reestablish civil government by the participation of loyal voters. The army was to "aid and assist the said provisional governor in carrying into effect this proclamation." Johnson also ordered soldiers "to abstain from in any way hindering, impeding, or discouraging the loyal people from the organization of a State government." Yet much remained unclear. A provisional governor of a state appointed by the president was an anomaly in American constitutional practice. A military force placed to whatever degree at the call of such an official was equally anomalous.

Controversies were bound to occur. Governors wrote to President Johnson complaining about military interference. Officers wrote to the Commanding General, Ulysses S. Grant, asking for instructions about the limits of their authority. In Mississippi, Governor William L. Sharkey and Gen. Henry W. Slocum clashed over the governor's desire to form a state militia independent of military control. A widespread subject of controversy was military arrests: Could commanders arrest civilians on their own initiative, or only in pursuance of a request from civilian officials for aid in effecting an arrest in a dangerous area? Law enforcement was made more complex by jurisdictional conflicts among (a) military commissions, (b) special Freedmen's Bureau courts designed to resolve labor contract disputes, and (c) local courts reopened by provisional governors. General Grant and Secretary of War Edwin M. Stanton supported the army in these conflicts, while President Johnson often sided with his political appointees, the provisional governors.

By September 1865, the number of troops in the South was down to 187,000. Distribution varied from 8,700 in Florida to 16,000 in Tennessee to 24,000 in Louisiana to 45,000 in Texas. A growing problem was the desire of white volunteer regiments to be mustered out, which left an increasing proportion of black regiments, organized late in the war, with a year or more left on their enlistments. By the end of 1865, when total troop strength had dropped to 88,000, black regiments outnumbered white ones by 11 to 1 in Mississippi, 6 to 1 in Tennessee, and 9 to 5 in Louisiana. There was a slight preponderance of black troops in Arkansas and Florida, and equal numbers in Alabama and Texas. Complaints from governors about mutual racial antipathy as well as negative reports about discipline from some commanding generals led to an increased discharge rate for black volunteer regiments during 1866.

In December 1865, Congress (which had been out of session since March) met for its new term, expressed dissatisfaction with the results of Johnson's program, and refused to readmit any seceded states to representation. This initiated a legislative struggle with Johnson over control of policy that lasted until March 1867. In consequence of the confusion in Washington, the army's role entered its third phase. The provisional governments remained in place, but congressional Republicans wanted more military supervision of them. Conflict with governors over appointment and removal of local officials increased. Passage of the Freedmen's Bureau Act meant continued military aid for that agency. Passage of the Civil Rights Act, signifying a congressional desire to supersede discriminatory state legislation and judicial practices, meant greater use of military courts, or at least military protection, for former slaves and white unionists. All the while numbers declined, from 39,000 troops in the South in April to 20,000 at year's end. In 1866, the total peacetime strength of the regular army was set at 58,000.

On 2 March 1867, Congress passed the First Reconstruction Act over Johnson's veto, thus establishing a program of "congressional Reconstruction." The army's role entered its fourth phase, which would continue in each state until such time, between the summer of 1868 and the spring of 1871, as the particular state gained readmission to Congress. During this phase, the army's direct power over civil affairs and southern politics reached its greatest extent. The First Reconstruction Act superseded all of the existing state governments, required the election of conventions to rewrite state constitutions, and mandated a new registration of voters under specified qualifications and the election of new governors and legislators. This political process occurred under total military supervision. Congress established five military districts and required the president to assign an army general to the command of each district.

That officer had the duty "to protect all persons in their rights of persons and property, to suppress insurrection, disorder, and violence, and to punish, or cause to be punished, all disturbers of the public peace and criminals." In a clarification of previous uncertainties, the commanding generals had specific permission to try civilians by military commission. Subsequent legislation allowed the generals to appoint the registration boards and control other aspects of the electoral process. They could also remove any civil official and need not accept the U.S. Attorney General's interpretation of their powers under the law.

Gen. Philip H. Sheridan in Louisiana and Gen. John Pope in Georgia removed governors as well as lesser officials. Pope gerrymandered electoral districts in order to control the results and sought to regulate the press by requiring official notices to be published only in papers that did not oppose congressional Reconstruction. The administration of Gen. John Schofield in Virginia was by comparison much less contentious.

By this legislation as well as other contemporary provisions, Congress had assigned the army an overtly political function. It had also made certain that the army would implement its views on Reconstruction and not those of the president. During the summer of 1867, Johnson removed Generals Sheridan, Pope, and Dan Sickles from their commands. His subsequent efforts to get Edwin M. Stanton out of the War Department led to his impeachment.

Congress readmitted several states to representation in the summer of 1868. Others followed in 1870 and 1871. Readmission began the fifth and last phase of army duties in the South, which would continue until the inauguration of Rutherford Hayes in the spring of 1877. Troop strength dropped from 18,000 in October 1868 (one-third on the Texas frontier) to 6,000 in the fall of 1876 (half in Texas). In 1869, a retrenchment-minded Congress once again cut the size of the regular army to less than 40,000 men.

Duties were more intermittent than continuous. Detachments went out to accompany federal revenue officers in search of illicit whiskey stills. General suppression of crime was also a task for the army, but now only at the request of civil authorities, federal or state. The amount of discretion left to the army in honoring these requests caused controversy; often the requests ended up in Washington for review and approval. In 1871, Gen. Alfred H. Terry reported that in the six states of his command, there had been more than 200 expeditions in aid of law enforcement that year. The army also provided the force behind a major effort to break the Ku Klux Klan in South Carolina during 1870–72. Around election time, military activity increased as small detachments visited troubled areas of the state to guard polls and discourage intimidation of voters. Congressional Reconstruction brought Republican state regimes to power, which often called for military aid in the period following readmission. The most continuous use of troops for this purpose was the protracted party struggle in Louisiana from 1872 to 1877.

The twelve years of Reconstruction saw frequent changes in policy, and with them, changes in the army's legal powers and functions. As an institution, the army was able to adjust to these changes, largely because officers saw themselves as administering policy rather than establishing it. This fit the established American tradition in civil-military relations, in spite of the executive-legislative conflict over army control in the Johnson years. The Posse Comitatus Act of 1878, reflecting the Reconstruction experience, further limited military enforcement of civil law. On the whole, military administration of federal policy was creditable to the institution of the U.S. Army despite errors of judgment and highly unusual circumstances.

APPENDIX 9: "SPANISH-AMERICAN WAR"

[Excerpts from "Spanish-American War." West's Encyclopedia of American Law. 2005. Retrieved 24 September 2013 from Encyclopedia.com: http:// www.encyclopedia.com/doc/1G2-3437704097.html]

The Spanish-American War of 1898 lasted only a few months...result[ing] in a U.S. victory that not only ended Spain's colonial rule in the Western Hemisphere but also marked the emergence of the United States as a world power, as it acquired Puerto Rico, the Philippines, and Guam. theodore roosevelt's military exploits in Cuba catapulted him onto the national stage and led to the vice presidency and, ultimately, the presidency.

The conflict had its origins in Spain's determined effort in the 1890s to destroy the Cuban independence movement. As the brutality of the Spanish authorities was graphically reported in U.S. newspapers, especially Joseph Pulitzer's *New York World* and William Randolph Hearst's *New York Journal,* the U.S. public began to support an independent Cuba.

In 1897 Spain proposed to resolve the conflict by granting partial autonomy to the Cubans, but the Cuban leaders continued to call for complete independence. In December 1897, the U.S. battleship *Maine* was sent to Havana to protect U.S. citizens and property. On the evening of February 15, 1898, the ship was sunk by a tremendous explosion, the cause of which was never determined. U.S. outrage at the loss of 266 sailors and the sensationalism of the New York press led to cries of "Remember the *Maine*" and demands that the United States intervene militarily in Cuba.

President william mckinley, who had originally opposed intervention, approved anApril 20 congressional resolution calling for immediate Spanish withdrawal from Cuba. This resolution precipitated a Spanish declaration of war against the United States on April 24. Congress immediately reciprocated and declared war on Spain on April 25, stating that the United States sought Cuban independence but not a foreign empire.

The war itself was brief due to the inferiority of the Spanish forces. On May 1, 1898, the Spanish fleet in Manila Bay in the Philippines was destroyed by the U.S. Navy under the command of Commodore George Dewey. On July 3, U.S. troops began a battle for the city of Santiago, Cuba. Roosevelt and his First Volunteer Cavalry, the "Rough Riders," led the charge up San Juan Hill; he emerged as one of the war's great heroes. With the sinking of the Spanish fleet off the coast of Cuba on July 3 and the capture of Santiago on July 17, the war was effectively over.

An armistice was signed on August 12, ending hostilities and directing that a peace conference be held in Paris by October. The parties signed the treaty of paris on December 12, 1898. Cuba was granted independence, and Spain agreed to pay the Cuban debt, which was estimated at $400 million. Spain gave the United States possession of the Philippines and also ceded Puerto Rico and Guam to the United States. Many members of the U.S. Senate opposed the treaty...concerned that the possession of the Philippines had made the United States an imperial power, claiming colonies just like European nations. This status as an imperial power, they argued, was contrary to traditional U.S. foreign policy, which was to refrain from external entanglements. The Treaty of Paris was ratified by only one vote on February 6, 1899.

APPENDIX 10: "PROGRESSIVISM"

[Excerpts from "progressivism." The Columbia Encyclopedia, 6th ed.. 2013. Retrieved 24 September 2013 from Encyclopedia.com: http://www.encyclopedia.com/doc/1E1-progrsvsm.html]

Progressivism... [is] a broadly based reform movement that reached its height early in the 20th cent. In the decades following the Civil War rapid industrialization transformed the United States. A national rail system was completed; agriculture was mechanized; the factory system spread; and cities grew rapidly in size and number. The progressive movement arose as a response to the vast changes brought by industrialization.

Urban Reform

Progressivism began in the cities, where the problems were most acute. Dedicated men and women of middle-class background moved into the slums and established settlement houses. Led by women such as Jane Addams in Chicago and Lillian Wald in New York City, they hoped to improve slum life through programs of self-help. Other reformers attacked corruption in municipal government; they formed nonpartisan leagues to defeat the entrenched bosses and their political machines. During the 1890s, reform mayors such as Hazen Pingree in Detroit, Samuel Jones in Toledo, and James Phelan in San Francisco were elected on platforms promising municipal ownership of public utilities, improved city services, and tenement housing codes. Urban reformers were often frustrated, however, because state legislatures, controlled by railroads and large corporations, obstructed the municipal struggle for home rule.

Reform on the State Level

Reformers turned to state politics, where progressivism reached its fullest expression. Robert La Follette's term as governor of Wisconsin (1901–6) was a model of progressive reform. He won from the legislature an antilobbying law directed at large corporations, a state banking control measure, and a direct primary law. Taxes on corporations were raised, a railroad commission was created to set rates, and a conservation commission was set up.

In state after state, progressives advocated a wide range of political, economic, and social reforms. They urged adoption of the secret ballot, direct primaries, the initiative, the referendum, and direct election of senators. They struck at the excessive power of corporate wealth by regulating railroads and utilities, restricting lobbying, limiting monopoly, and raising corporate taxes. To correct the worst features of industrialization, progressives advocated worker's compensation, child labor laws, minimum wage and maximum hours legislation (especially for women workers), and widows' pensions.

Reform on the National Level

As progressives gained strength on the state level, they turned to national politics. Little headway was made, however, since conservatives controlled the Senate. Some progress was made against the trusts during Theodore Roosevelt's administration, and Congress passed two bills regulating railroads, the Elkins Act (1903) and the Hepburn Act (1906). The exposés of business practices by the muckrakers aroused public opinion. The Pure Food and Drug Act and the Meat Inspection Act were passed (1906) to eliminate the worst practices of the food industry. Although Roosevelt supported the progressive drive for regulation of corporations and for social-welfare legislation, Congress remained adamant.

Roosevelt's successor, William Howard Taft, was a determined opponent of progressive reform; in 1911 progressives, whose ranks had been swelled by middle-class professionals, small businessmen, and farmers, formed the National Progressive Republican League to prevent Taft's renomination. When this failed, progressives united in a third party (see Progressive party) and nominated (1912) Roosevelt for President. Although Roosevelt was defeated, the new President, Woodrow Wilson, sponsored many progressive measures. The Federal Reserve Act of 1913 reformed the currency system; the Clayton Antitrust Act and the Federal Trade Commission Act (1914) extended government regulation of big business; and the Keating-Owen Act (1916) restricted child labor.

Progressivism's Legacy

America's entry into World War I diverted the energy of reformers, and after the war progressivism virtually died....Most of the social-welfare measures advocated by progressives had to await the New Deal years for passage.

APPENDIX 11: "WORLD WAR I"

[Excerpts from "World War I." Dictionary of American History. 2003. Retrieved 24 September 2013 from Encyclopedia.com: http://www.encyclopedia.com/doc/ 1G2-3401804601.html]

The United States did not enter World War I until April 1917, although the conflict had begun in August 1914. After an intense period of military buildup and imperial competition, war broke out in Europe between Germany and Austria-Hungary (the Central Powers) and Britain, France, and Russia (the Allies). Turkey quickly joined the Central Powers and Italy joined the Allies in 1915.

Prelude to Involvement

...President Woodrow Wilson issued a declaration of neutrality. He was committed to maintaining open use of the Atlantic for trade with all the European belligerents. However, British naval supremacy almost eliminated American trade with Germany while shipments to the Allies soared. To counter this trend, German U-boats (submarines) torpedoed U.S. merchant vessels bound for Allied ports. In May 1915, Germans sunk the British passenger ship *Lusitania,* killing 128 Americans. Strong protest from Wilson subdued the submarine campaign, but it would emerge again as the war ground on and became more desperate. In late January 1917, Germany announced it would destroy all ships heading to Britain. Although Wilson broke off diplomatic ties with Germany, he still hoped to avert war by arming merchant vessels as a deterrent. Nevertheless, Germany began sinking American ships immediately.

In February 1917, British intelligence gave the United States government a decoded telegram from Germany's foreign minister, Arthur Zimmerman, that had been intercepted en route to his ambassador to Mexico. The Zimmerman Telegram authorized the ambassador to offer Mexico...portions of the Southwest it had lost to the United States in the 1840s if it joined the Central Powers. But because Wilson had run for reelection in 1916 on a very popular promise to keep the United States out of the European war, he had to handle the telegram very carefully. Wilson did not publicize it at first, only releasing the message to the press in March after weeks of German attacks on American ships had turned public sentiment toward joining the Allies.

Gearing Up for War: Raising Troops and Rallying Public Opinion

On 2 April 1917, Wilson asked Congress for a declaration of war and four days later all but six senators and fifty representatives voted for a war resolution. The Selective Service Act that was passed the following month, along with an extraordinary number of volunteers, built up the army from less than 250,000 to four million over the course of the conflict. General John Pershing was appointed head of the American Expeditionary Force (AEF) and led the first troops to France during the summer. Initially, the nation was woefully unprepared to fight so large a war so far from American soil. The task of reorganizing government and industry to coordinate a war and then of recruiting, training, equipping, and shipping out massive numbers of soldiers was daunting and would proceed slowly. The first serious U.S. military action would not come until April 1918, one year after declaration of war. It would take a gargantuan national effort, one that would forever change the government and its relationship to the citizenry, to get those troops into combat.

Although there is strong evidence that the war was broadly supported—and certainly Americans volunteered and bought Liberty Bonds in droves—the epic scale of the undertaking and the pressure of time led the government, in an unprecedented campaign, to sell the war effort through a massive propaganda blitz. Wilson picked George Creel, a western newspaper editor, to form the Committee on Public Information (CPI). This organization was charged with providing the press with carefully selected information on the progress of the war. It also worked with the advertising industry to produce eyecatching and emotional propaganda for various agencies involved in the war effort in order to win maximum cooperative enthusiasm form the public. Its largest enterprise was the Four Minute Men program, which sent more than 75,000 speakers to over 750,000 public events to rouse the patriotism of as many as 314 million spectators over the course of the war. The CPI recruited mainly prominent white businessmen and community leaders; however, it did set up a Women's Division and also courted locally prominent African Americans to speak at black gatherings.

Gearing Up for War: The Economy and Labor

The government needed patriotic cooperation, for it was completely unequipped to enforce many of the new regulations it adopted. It also had to maximize the productive resources of the nation to launch the U.S. war effort and prop up flagging allies. The War Industries Board was charged with gearing up the economy to war production, but it lacked coercive authority. Even the Overman Act of May 1918, which gave the president broad powers to commandeer industries if necessary, failed to convince capitalists to retool completely toward the war effort. The government only took control of one industry, the railroads, in December 1917, and made it quite clear that the measure was only a temporary necessity. In all other industries, it was federal investment—not control—that achieved results. The Emergency Fleet Corporation pumped over $3 billion into the nation's dormant shipbuilding industry during the war era. Overall, the effort to raise production was too little and too late for maximizing the nation's military clout. American production was just hitting stride as the war ended, but the threat that it represented did help convince an exhausted Germany to surrender.

The government also sought the cooperation of the American Federation of Labor (AFL) and involved its top officials in the war production effort, but very low unemployment emboldened union workers and it became difficult for the leadership to control the rank and file. Many workers connected Wilson's war goals—democracy and self-determination for nations—to struggles for a voice in their workplaces through union representation. However, the number of striking workers was lower in 1917 and 1918 than in 1916. The government hastily created labor arbitration boards and eventually formed a National War Labor Board (NWLB) in April 1918. The government had considerable success in resolving disputes and convincing employers to at least temporarily give some ground to the unions. When this novel arbitration framework disappeared along with government contracts in 1919, workers participated in the largest strike wave in the nation's history—over four million participated in walkouts during that year.

Women and African Americans in the War

For women workers the war also raised hopes, but as with labor as a whole, they were dashed after the conflict. The number of women working as domestic servants and in laundering or garment making declined sharply during the war, while opportunities grew just as dramatically in office, industrial, commercial, and transportation work. The very limited place of women in the economy had opened up and government propaganda begged women to take jobs. However, few of these new opportunities, and even then only the least attractive of them, went to nonwhite women. Mainly confined to low-skilled work, many women were let go when the postwar economy dipped or were replaced by returning soldiers. Although women did gain, and hold on to, a more prominent place in the AFL, they were still only 10 percent of the membership in 1920. The government made some attempts through the NWLB to protect the rights of working women, although it backed off after the war. But women fought on their own behalf on the suffrage front and finally achieved the right to vote in 1920.

African Americans also made some gains but suffered a terrible backlash for them. There were ninety-six lynchings of blacks during 1917 and 1918 and seventy in 1919 alone. Blacks were moving out of the South in massive numbers during the war years, confronting many white communities in the North with a substantial nonwhite presence for the first time. Northward migration by blacks averaged only 67,000 per decade from 1870 through 1910 and then exploded to 478,000 during the 1910s. This Great Migration gave blacks access to wartime factory jobs that paid far better than agricultural work in the South, but like white women, they primarily did lowskilled work and were generally rejected by the union movement. The hatred that many of these migrants faced in the North forced them into appalling ghettos and sometimes led to bloodshed. In July 1917, a race riot in East St. Louis, Illinois, left thirty-nine African Americans dead. The recently formed NAACP championed justice and democratic rights for African Americans at a time when black soldiers were helping to guarantee them for the peoples of Europe. Although job opportunities would recede after the war, the new racial diversity outside the South would not—and neither would the fight for equal rights.

Repression and the War

The fragility of a war effort that relied on a workforce of unprecedented diversity and on cooperation from emboldened unions led the federal government to develop for the first time a substantial intelligence-gathering capability for the purpose of suppressing elements it thought might destabilize the system. The primary targets were anti-capitalist radicals and enemy aliens (German and Austro-Hungarian immigrants). The former group was targeted through the Espionage Act of June 1917, which was amended by the Sedition Act in May 1918 after the Bolshevik Revolution in Russia convinced the government to seek even wider powers to control public speech. The Department of Justice, through its U.S. attorneys and Bureau of Investigation field agents, cooperated with local and state authorities to suppress radical organizers. Many government agencies developed at least some intelligence capacity and the private, but government sanctioned, American Protective League recruited perhaps 300,000 citizen-spies to keep tabs on their fellow Americans. In this climate of suspicion, German-speaking aliens had the most cause to be afraid. War propaganda dehumanized Germans and blasted their culture and language. Well over a half-million enemy aliens were screened by the Department of Justice and were restricted in their mobility and access to military and war production sites. Several thousand enemy aliens deemed disloyal were interned until the conflict was over.

American Soldiers in Battle

The end of the war was nowhere in sight when U.S. troops first saw significant fighting in the spring of 1918, after the new Bolshevik government in Russia pulled out of the war in March and Germany switched its efforts to the western front. Under British and French pressure, General Pershing allowed his troops to be blended with those of the Allies —ending his dream of the AEF as an independent fighting force. Now under foreign command, American troops helped stop the renewed German offensive in May and June. The First U.S. Army was given its own mission in August: to push the Germans back to the southeast and northwest of Verdun and then seize the important railroad facilities at Sedan. The campaign got under way in September and American troops succeeded in removing the Germans from the southeast of Verdun, although the latter were already evacuating that area. The Meuse-Argonne offensive to the northwest of Verdun was launched in late September and proved to be much more bloody. Although the German position was heavily fortified, well over a million American soldiers simply overwhelmed all resistance. This massive and relentless operation convinced the German command that its opportunity to defeat the Allies before American troops and industry were fully ready to enter the fray had been lost. As exhausted as the United States was fresh, the Central Powers surrendered on 11 November 1918.

In the end, two million American troops went to France and three-quarters of them saw combat. Some 60,000 died in battle and over 200,000 were wounded. An additional 60,000 died of disease, many from the influenza pandemic that killed over twenty million across the globe in 1918 and 1919. Many surviving combatants suffered psychological damage, known as shell shock, from the horrors of trench warfare. The casualties would have been far greater had America entered the war earlier or been prepared to deploy a large army more quickly.

Wilson hoped that after the war the United States would become part of the League of Nations that was forming in Europe to ensure that collective responsibility replaced competitive alliances. But America was retreating inward, away from the postwar ruin and revolutionary chaos of Europe. The government was suppressing radicals at home with unprecedented furor in 1919 and 1920 in what is known as the Red Scare. Progressive wartime initiatives that further involved the government in the lives of its citizens withered against this reactionary onslaught. But the notion of government coordination of a national effort to overcome crisis had been born, and the Great Depression and World War II would see this new commitment reemerge, strengthened.

APPENDIX 12: "THE NEW DEAL"

[Excerpts from "New Deal." The Columbia Encyclopedia, 6th ed.. 2013. Retrieved 24 September 2013 from Encyclopedia.com: http://www.encyclopedia.com/doc/ 1E1-NewDeal.html]

[The] New Deal, in U.S. history, [was the] term for the domestic reform program of the administration of Franklin Delano Roosevelt; it was first used by Roosevelt in his speech accepting the Democratic party nomination for President in 1932. The New Deal is generally considered to have consisted of two phases.

The first phase (1933–34) attempted to provide recovery and relief from the Great Depression through programs of agricultural and business regulation, inflation, price stabilization, and public works. Meeting (1933) in special session, Congress established numerous emergency organizations, notably the National Recovery Administration (NRA), the Federal Deposit Insurance Corporation (FDIC), the Agricultural Adjustment Administration (AAA), the Civilian Conservation Corps, and the Public Works Administration. Congress also instituted farm relief, tightened banking and finance regulations, and founded the Tennessee Valley Authority. Later Democratic Congresses devoted themselves to expanding and modifying these laws. In 1934, Congress founded the Securities and Exchange Commission and the Federal Communications Commission and passed the Trade Agreements Act, the National Housing Act, and various currency acts.

The second phase of the New Deal (1935–41), while continuing with relief and recovery measures, provided for social and economic legislation to benefit the mass of working people. The social security system was established in 1935, the year the National Youth Administration and Work Projects Administration were set up. The Fair Labor Standards Act was passed in 1938. The Revenue Acts of 1935, 1936, and 1937 provided measures to democratize the federal tax structure. A number of New Deal measures were invalidated by the Supreme Court, however; in 1935 the NRA was struck down and the following year the AAA was invalidated. The President unsuccessfully sought to reorganize the Supreme Court. Meanwhile, other laws were substituted for legislation that had been declared unconstitutional.

The New Deal, which had received the endorsement of agrarian, liberal, and labor groups, met with increasing criticism. The speed of reform slackened after 1937, and there was growing Republican opposition to the huge public spending, high taxes, and centralization of power in the executive branch of government; within the Democratic party itself there was strong disapproval from the "old guard" and from disgruntled members of the Brain Trust. As the prospect of war in Europe increased, the emphasis of government shifted to foreign affairs. There was little retreat from reform, however; at the end of World War II, most of the New Deal legislation was still intact, and it remains the foundation for American social policy.

APPENDIX 13: "WORLD WAR II & THE POSTWAR WORLD"

[Excerpts from "World War II." International Encyclopedia of the Social Sciences. 2008. Retrieved 24 September 2013 from Encyclopedia.com: http:// www.encyclopedia.com/doc/1G2-3045303000.html]

World War II was a military conflict from 1939 to 1945....considered to have been the largest and deadliest war in world history, killing 62 million people on the battlefield, in massive bombings of civilians in cities, and by genocide. There were two hostile camps—the Axis Powers of Germany, Italy, Japan, Romania, Bulgaria, Hungary, Croatia, Slovakia, Finland (cobelligerent), Thailand, and others; and the Allied Powers of the British Empire and Commonwealth (including India, Canada, Australia and New Zealand), France, the United States, the Soviet Union, China, the Netherlands, Norway, Belgium, Poland, and others. The global reach of the empires of France, Italy, and Britain meant that non-European areas became directly involved with battles fought in Africa, the Middle East, Europe, and Asia. Organized civilian resistance movements in occupied countries (notably Yugoslavia, France, and Greece) made important contributions to the Allied war effort. The economic effects of the war have been estimated at $1 trillion in 1945 (approximately $10.5 trillion in 2005 terms). It is the only time in history that nuclear weapons were used (by the United States against Japan). The end of World War II resulted in the partitioning of Europe into East (ruled by Communist governments under the sphere of influence of the Soviet Union aligned under the Council for Mutual Economic Assistance, or Comecon, and the Warsaw Pact) and West (with democratic governments receiving economic reconstruction aid through the U.S. Marshall Plan aligned under NATO), the U.S. occupation of Japan, and new international organizations such as the United Nations, the International Monetary Fund, and the World Bank. The immediate postwar era also saw the rise of European integration efforts with the formation of the European Coal and Steel Community and the European Economic Community, which would develop into the European Union by the end of the century, and the beginning of the cold war between the United States and the Soviet Union that would mark the second half of the twentieth century.

EXPANSIONISM AND ECONOMIC CONDITIONS

Territorial expansion of Germany and Italy began before any military hostilities. The most noted example of territorial demands made by Hitler's Germany is Czechoslovakia (where Germans comprised one-third of the population), followed by German-speaking Austria. But the Reich sought further expansion. Many in Germany never accepted the creation of

Poland following World War I, and they focused territorial demands on the Polish Corridor, a narrow strip of land separating East Prussia from Germany that allowed Poland access to the Baltic Sea, but also sought broader territory that would expand Germany to a common border with Russia. In 1935 Germany regained the Saar region, in March 1936 it reoccupied the Rhineland, and in 1937 it achieved *Anschluss* (union) with Austria. Italy's fascist leader, Benito Mussolini, also hoped to acquire territory, particularly at the expense of France, Albania, and Greece, to create a New Roman Empire. In 1934 Italy moved against Abyssinia on the border of Italian Somaliland and Ethiopia. Territory was also an important factor in the war in Asia. One of the most often cited reasons for Japan's aggression in Asia is that nation's need for the raw materials naturally lacking in its own territory. Thus Japan, the only burgeoning industrial economy in Asia at the time, invaded first Manchuria, then other areas throughout the Asian mainland, and finally the Western Pacific in order to secure necessary natural resources such as oil and iron ore.

The economic effects of the Treaty of Versailles and the Great Depression were important factors in radicalizing German politics. In April 1921 Germany was presented with a reparations bill of $33 billion by the victorious allies of World War I. Reparations payments hobbled the weakened German economy, causing rapidly rising inflation and a dramatically depreciating currency. France refused Germany's request for a postponement, Germany defaulted on the war reparations in 1923, and the French army occupied part of the Ruhr (the German industrial zone). Hyperinflation ensued as the German currency, the mark, plummeted to 4 billion marks to the dollar (from 75 marks to the dollar in 1921 and 18,000 in January 1923), eliminating life savings and making salaries worthless. Groceries cost billions of marks (wheelbarrows of currency were needed for a single loaf of bread) and hunger riots broke out. In September 1923 the German government resumed reparations payments, inciting bitter popular resentment and paving the way for extremist political groups such as the Nazi Party (National Socialist Party).

IDEOLOGY, NATIONALISM, AND MILITARISM

Under the terms of the Treaty of Versailles, the German army was allowed to remain intact and was not forced to admit defeat by surrendering. The German general staff supported the idea that the army had not been defeated on the battlefield and could have fought on to victory were they not betrayed at home (the *Dolchstosslegende*, or "stab-in-the-back legend") by German politicians who signed the November 1918 armistice (the "November Criminals"). The theory became very popular among Germans: Adolf Hitler, a World War I veteran, became obsessed with this idea, laying blame firmly on Jews and Marxists for undermining Germany's war effort. The Nazi Party won 230 of 608 seats in the Reichstag (German parliament) in January 1933; within six months Hitler was elected chancellor. The Nazis pledged to first restore Germany to its rightful place in Europe, and then to seek world power.

Racism and anti-Semitism characterized the Nazi Party, which organized official boycotts of Jewish shops and professional men and the opening of the first concentration camp in Dachau, outside Munich, in March 1933. In September 1935 the Nuremberg Laws relegated Jews to separate, second-class status and prohibited intermarriage and sexual relations with Aryan Germans. In November 1938 Nazis orchestrated a nationwide pogrom on Jews following the murder of a German diplomatic assistant in the German embassy in Paris by a French Jew. Jewish homes, shops, and 191 synagogues were destroyed and 20,000 Jews were arrested on *Kristallnacht* ("Night of Broken Glass"). German anti-Semitism culminated in the Holocaust.

Although technically an absolute monarchy under Emperor Hirohito, Japan was politically dominated by a group of militaristic generals in charge of the most powerful army in Asia at the time. Japanese militarism was accompanied by racism, toward both Europeans and other Asians, especially Chinese and Koreans. Anyone who was not Japanese was considered inferior and treated as such. One example of Japanese violent racism is General Shiro Ishii's Unit 731 experiments in Pingfan in Harbin, China, in which as many as 10,000 Chinese, Korean, and Russian prisoners of war and civilians were subjected to brutal experiments in vivisection, germ warfare, and weapons testing.

APPEASEMENT

Britain and France followed an early policy of accommodation and compromise in Germany's favor in the hope of avoiding another war, known as the "policy of appeasement"; many thought the Treaty of Versailles imposed unreasonable demands on Germany. In June 1935 the Anglo-German Naval Agreement was signed, signaling Britain's unwillingness to defend the Versailles settlement. In March 1936 German military reoccupation of the Rhineland (demilitarized under the Versailles Treaty) met with no opposition from France and thus successfully challenged France's willingness to defend the Versailles settlement. In January 1937 Hitler publicly broke with the Treaty of Versailles.

Neville Chamberlain, the prime minister of Britain from 1937 to 1940, is known for adopting a policy of appeasement in an attempt to preserve the peace and buy time for any major rearmament. In September 1938 Britain, France, and Italy agreed at the Munich Conference to grant Czechoslovakia's Sudetenland to Germany. In return, Hitler gave Chamberlain his personal word on future cooperation. The Munich Pact is considered the height of appeasement. On his return to London, Chamberlain stated: "We regard the agreement signed last night [Munich Pact] and the Anglo-German Naval Agreement as symbolic of the desire of our two peoples never to go to war with one another again.… My good friends, for the second time in our history, a British Prime Minister has returned from Germany bringing peace with honor. I believe it is peace for our time.… Go home and get a nice quiet sleep." Chamberlain resigned in 1940 and was replaced by Winston Churchill, who led Britain to the end of the war. The Molotov-Ribbentrop Pact of nonaggression signed by Germany and the Soviet Union in 1939 is also considered by some historians as an act of appeasement or as an attempt by Joseph Stalin to buy time to prepare for an impending German attack on the Soviet Union.

U.S. ENTRY INTO THE WAR

Since 1940 the United States had allowed the covert operation in China of the American Volunteer Group, or "Chennault's Flying Tigers," to assist the Chinese war effort. The Flying Tigers destroyed an estimated 115 Japanese aircraft, sunk numerous Japanese ships, and participated in the Burma land campaign. U.S. president Franklin D. Roosevelt cut exports of oil and scrap iron to Japan in 1941. Japan planned and executed a strike on Pearl Harbor, Hawaii, on Sunday, December 7, 1941, to cripple the U.S. Pacific fleet and consolidate oil fields in Southeast Asia. The attack on Pearl Harbor achieved military surprise and severely damaged the U.S. navy, and it remains the largest military attack on U.S. soil.

Following the Japanese attack on Pearl Harbor, Hitler declared war on the United States on December 11, 1941, in the hope that Japan would assist Germany by attacking the Soviet Union (it did not). Pearl Harbor, in conjunction with Hitler's declaration of war, gave Roosevelt the domestic support he needed to join the war in Europe and Asia without meaningful opposition from Congress. Many historians consider this an important turning point of the war in Europe, marking the formation of a grand alliance of powerful nations (the United Kingdom, the United States, and the Soviet Union) against Germany.

POSTWAR DIVISION, OCCUPATION, AND RECONSTRUCTION

After World War II, Europe was informally partitioned into Western Europe and Eastern Europe under the NATO and Warsaw Pact military alliances and the Marshall Plan and Comecon economic arrangements. Germany was formally divided into the states of the Federal Republic of Germany (F.D.R., or West Germany) and the German Democratic Republic (G.D.R., or East Germany). Allied troops remained in Germany for decades following the war. Following German reunification in October 1990, the new united Germany still had Soviet troops stationed in its eastern provinces.

The U.S. Marshall Plan intended to rebuild the European economy and promote European unity while thwarting the political appeal of communism. For Western Europe, economic aid ended the dollar shortage and stimulated private investment for postwar reconstruction. The Marshall Plan required European states to work together to utilize the funds, an obligation that later facilitated the formation of the European Economic Community.

The Council for Mutual Economic Assistance (COMECON, Comecon, CMEA, or CEMA) was formed in 1949 as an economic organization of Communist states. Its original members were the Soviet Union, Bulgaria, Romania, Hungary, Czechoslovakia, Albania, the German Democratic Republic, and Poland. Albania, Hungary, Czechoslovakia, Bulgaria, and Romania, which were allied with the Axis Powers during the war, came under the Soviet sphere of influence, with their Communist governments joining the Soviet-led Comecon economic and trade area, as did Poland. In 1950 East Germany joined Comecon. (Other members included Mongolia [1962], Cuba [1972], and Vietnam [1978]. Yugoslavia [1964] was an associate member; other Communist countries or Soviet-friendly governments were observers.) Comecon members had common approaches to state economic ownership and planned management, and political regimes that espoused the ideologies of Marxism-Leninism. In 1949 the ruling Communist parties of the founding states were also linked internationally through the Cominform, the Communist Information Bureau, which established information exchanges between members. The East European members of Comecon were also militarily allied with the Soviet Union in the Warsaw Pact.

In Asia, the U.S. military occupation of Japan led to Japan's democratization. China's civil war continued during and after World War II, culminating in the establishment of the Communist People's Republic of China. Europe's Asian colonies India, Indonesia, and Vietnam started toward independence.

LEGACY OF WORLD WAR II

One of the most important legacies of World War II was the creation of a set of international institutions to provide for international governance of global security and monetary relations. Postwar security and economic institutions were created exclusively by the victorious Allied Powers and reflected the postwar power structure. The term *United Nations* was first coined by Roosevelt during the war to refer to the Allies. On January 1, 1942, the Declaration by the United Nations committed the Allies to the principles of the Atlantic Charter and pledged them not to seek a separate peace with the Axis Powers. Thereafter, the Allies used the term *United Nations Fighting Forces* to refer to their alliance. The United Nations institutions were created during the war itself to govern international relations after the war.

The initial ideas for a global security organization were first elaborated at wartime Allied conferences in Moscow, Cairo, and Tehran in 1943. During August to October 1944 representatives from France, Britain, the Soviet Union, China, and the United States met in Dumbarton Oaks in Washington, D.C., to prepare plans for an organization that would maintain peace and security, and economic and social cooperation. The formal monetary conference predated the security conference: The United Nations Monetary and Financial Conference of July 1 to 22, 1944 (called the Bretton Woods conference), took place in Bretton Woods, New Hampshire, with 730 delegates from 45 Allied countries. It established the Bretton Woods system of international exchange-rate management that remained in place until the mid-1970s, and it produced two separate institutions (called the Bretton Woods institutions) to monitor, regulate, and facilitate international monetary affairs and finance in the post–World War II era. The World Bank and the International Monetary Fund, both headquartered in Washington, D.C., have had lasting influence on the international political economy since their inception. The International Monetary Fund was entrusted with overseeing the global financial system by monitoring exchange rates and balance of payments, providing liquidity, and offering technical and financial assistance. The World Bank, or International Bank for Reconstruction and Development (IBRD), was entrusted with providing finance such as grants or loans at preferential rates, technical assistance, and advice to countries for the purpose of economic development and poverty reduction, and for encouraging and safeguarding international investment. Although the World Bank's activities have evolved to focus on developing countries, the first loan issued by the World Bank was approved on May 9, 1947, to France in the amount of $250 million for postwar reconstruction; this remains its largest loan to date in real terms. World Bank loans and grants provide financing to countries that have no access to international capital markets.

The United Nations Conference on International Organizations opened at the Fairmont Hotel in San Francisco on April 25, 1945, with fifty nations and some nongovernmental organizations represented. Initially referred to as the United Nations Organization, the UN was comprised of several administrative bodies (General Assembly, Secretariat, Economic and Social Council, Trusteeship Council, and the International Court of Justice to adjudicate disputes among nations), the most prominent of which is the Security Council, where members resolve action on issues of war and aggression. (For example, all UN peacekeeping operations must be approved by the Security Council.) The United Nations Charter was signed on June 26, 1945, and the UN, headquartered in New York City, came into existence in October 1945 after the charter had been ratified by the five permanent members of the Security Council and a majority of signatory states. It replaced the League of Nations, which had been founded after World War I and had proved ineffective at preventing war and securing peace and order. The structure of the UN reflected the World War II victory, with the most powerful Allies—the United Kingdom, France, the United States, the Soviet Union, and China—holding the only permanent seats in the UN Security Council with veto power over decisions. The World Bank and International Monetary Fund came into existence a few months after the UN, in December 1945 following international ratification of the Articles of Agreement (called the Bretton Woods agreements).

Another legacy of World War II saw the development and use of many new technologies, including long-range missiles, jet aircraft, radar, and atomic (nuclear) weapons. Nuclear weapons were created in the top-secret Manhattan Project in the United States (with assistance from the United Kingdom and Canada) by an international team that included émigré scientists from Central Europe, initially out of fear that Germany would develop them first. (The Soviet Union became the second nuclear power in 1949.) Nuclear weapons have only been used twice in the history of warfare, both in the closing days of World War II by the United States against Japan, the first on August 6, 1945, on the Japanese city of Hiroshima, and the second on August 9, 1945, on the Japanese city of Nagasaki. Each use comprised the dropping of a single airborne atomic bomb (atom bomb, A-bomb, or simply "the bomb"). The bombs killed an estimated 200,000 people (mostly civilians) instantly, and twice as many later through the effects of radiation. The advent of nuclear weapons came only weeks after the signing of the UN Charter, providing immediate impetus to concepts of arms limitation and disarmament. The first resolution of the first meeting of the UN General Assembly on January 24, 1946, was "The Establishment of a Commission to Deal with the Problems Raised by the Discovery of Atomic Energy," which called upon the commission to make specific proposals for "the elimination from national armaments of atomic weapons and of all other major weapons adaptable to mass destruction."

World War II atrocities and genocide in both Europe and Asia led to a consensus that nations must work to prevent such tragedies in the future. Another early objective of the United Nations was to create a legal framework for considering and acting on complaints about human rights violations. The UN Charter obliges all member nations to promote "universal respect for, and observance of, human rights" and to take "joint and separate action" to that end. The Universal Declaration of Human Rights was adopted by the UN General Assembly in 1948 as a common standard of achievement for all.

World War II resulted in a fundamental shift in global power from the weakened British Empire to the United States and the Soviet Union. Almost immediately following World War II, a protracted geopolitical, ideological, and economic struggle emerged between two of the most powerful Allied Powers—the United States and the Soviet Union. The struggle was called the cold war because it did not involve direct armed conflict between the United States and the Soviet Union, although each formed an opposing military alliance in Europe and engaged in the biggest arms race (including nuclear weapons) in history. The cold war lasted from about 1947 to the collapse of communism in the late 1980s, the fall of the Berlin Wall in 1989, and the dissolution of the Soviet Union in 1991.

The North Atlantic Treaty Organization (NATO, or the North Atlantic Alliance, Atlantic Alliance, or Western Alliance) was established with the signing of the North Atlantic Treaty on April 4, 1949, in Washington, D.C., for the purpose of collective security of the members, binding each to a military alliance with all the others. The treaty avoids identification of an enemy or concrete measures of common defense, but the implied adversary was the Soviet Union. This marked a significant change in the isolationist tendencies of the United States and signaled the lasting involvement of the United States in European security affairs. It also formally divided the World War II Allies in the West from the Soviet Union by creating a new military alliance composed largely of World War II Allied Powers. The original members of NATO were the United States, France, Britain, Belgium, Luxembourg, Netherlands, Portugal, Norway, Denmark, and Iceland (West Germany was not incorporated until 1955, after the formation of the Warsaw Pact).

In 1955 the Warsaw Pact (Warsaw Treaty, or Treaty of Friendship, Cooperation, and Mutual Assistance) was established as a military organization of Eastern and Central European Communist states to counter the threat perceived by NATO. Its members consisted of the Soviet Union, Bulgaria, Czechoslovakia, Hungary, Poland, Romania, East Germany (in 1956), and Albania (which withdrew in 1968). Similar to the NATO members, the Warsaw Pact signatories pledged to defend each other if one of them was attacked. It is noteworthy that the members of the Warsaw Pact consisted of Axis Powers as well as Allied Powers (the Soviet Union and Poland). The Warsaw Pact officially dissolved in 1991. Although not a member of NATO, the Axis Power Japan became allied with the United States. Although not a member of the Warsaw Pact, the Allied Power China was friendly to the Soviet Union. Countries such as Yugoslavia, Switzerland, Austria, India, Sweden, and Finland conspicuously maintained their neutrality by participation in the Non-Aligned Movement.

APPENDIX 14: "THE MARSHALL PLAN"

[Excerpts from "Marshall Plan." West's Encyclopedia of American Law. 2005. Retrieved 24 September 2013 from Encyclopedia.com: http:// www.encyclopedia.com/doc/1G2-3437702837.html]

After world war ii, Europe was devastated and urgently needed an organized plan for reconstruction and economic and technical aid. The Marshall Plan was initiated in 1947 to meet this need.

The originator of the plan, U.S. Secretary of State George C. Marshall, introduced it in a speech at Harvard University on June 5, 1947...point[ing] out two basic reasons for providing aid to Europe: the United States sought the reestablishment of the European countries as independent nations capable of conducting valuable trade with the United States; and the threat of a Communist takeover was more prevalent in countries that were suffering economic depression.

In 1947 a preliminary conference to discuss the terms of the program convened in Paris. The Soviet Union was invited to attend but subsequently withdrew from the program, as did other Soviet countries.

Sixteen European countries eventually participated, and, in July 1947, the Committee for European Economic Cooperation was established to allow representatives from member countries to draft a report that listed their requirements for food, supplies, and technical assistance for a four-year period.

The Committee for European Economic Cooperation subsequently became the Organization of European Economic Cooperation, an expanded and permanent organization that was responsible for submitting petitions for aid. In 1948, Congress passed the Economic Cooperation Act (62 Stat. 137), establishing funds for the Marshall Plan to be administered under the Economic Cooperation Administration, which was directed by Paul G. Hoffman.

Between 1948 and 1952, the sixteen-member countries received more than $13 billion dollars in aid under the Marshall Plan. The plan was generally regarded as a success that led to industrial and agricultural production, while stifling the Communist movement....

APPENDIX 15: "THE KOREAN WAR"

[Excerpts from "Korean War." Gale Encyclopedia of U.S. Economic History. 1999. Retrieved 24 September 2013 from Encyclopedia.com: http:// www.encyclopedia.com/doc/1G2-3406400502.html]

In 1948 as part of the boundary adjustments following World War II...Korea was supposedly temporarily divided for occupation by the Soviet Union and the United States as victorious former allies against Japan. The Korean peninsula, whose reclusive history in the seventeenth and eighteenth centuries led it to be called the "Hermit Kingdom," had been under Japanese control since the end of the Russo-Japanese War (1904–1905). The division following World War II was at the 38th parallel, a temporary line of demarcation with no other cultural or geographic significance. Like the artificial divisions of Germany and of Berlin in 1945, as well as the supposedly temporary division of North and South Vietnam in 1954, this bifurcation of the Korean nation was a result of the Cold War rather than internal developments.

In their zone lying north of the 38th parallel, the Soviets organized a socialist regime under the Communist Party. Established in 1948 as the Democratic People's Republic of Korea, the regime was headed by Kim Il Sung, a long-time leader of the Communist Party. In the South, various factions vied for power, until the party of the "father of Korean nationalism," Syngman Rhee, won a United Nations–sponsored election. On August 15, 1948, Rhee became President of the Republic of Korea. His regime was about as dictatorial as that in North Korea, and was implicated in corruption and in the repression of internal political opposition.

Both Korean governments were determined to achieve unification on their own terms. Shortly after partition, North Korea supported large-scale guerrilla incursions into the south, and retaliatory raids by South Korean forces kept the divided country in a state of crisis. Despite this situation, American troops were withdrawn in June 1949, leaving behind only a small group of technical advisers. South Korea, whose army was small, poorly trained, and poorly equipped, faced an adversary with an army of 135,000 men, equipped with modern Russian weapons, and between 150 and 200 combat airplanes. Although South Korean leaders and some Americans feared that North Korea might attack across the 38th parallel at any time, Secretary of State Dean Acheson, declared that Korea was not within the "defensive perimeter" of America's vital interests in the Far East.

The attack came on June 25, 1950. North Korean armed forces—armored units and mechanized divisions supported by massive artillery—struck without warning across the demarcation line. Meeting little resistance, within thirty-six hours North Korean tanks were approaching the outer suburbs of Seoul, the capital of South Korea.

Contrary to Korean and Soviet expectations, the United States reacted swiftly and with great determination. Immediately after the attack the United States requested that the UN Security Council hold a special session which passed a unanimous resolution calling for the end of hostilities and the withdrawal of North Korean forces to their former positions north of the 38th parallel. The Soviet Union would probably have vetoed such a resolution but the Soviets were boycotting the Security Council to protest the failure of the UN to include Communist China in its deliberations. In any case, the resolution was ignored by the North Koreans and the Security Council met again on June 27 and passed another resolution recommending that "the members of the United Nations furnish such assistance to the Republic of Korea as may be necessary to repel the armed attack." On June 27, U.S. President Harry S Truman committed U.S. Air and Naval forces to the "police action" (a war was never formally declared) as well as ground forces stationed in Japan.

The North Koreans, however, continued their advance. By the end of June, more than half of the Republic of Korea (ROK) Army had been destroyed, and American units were forced to fight countless rear-guard actions in the retreat southward. In early August, a defense perimeter was created around the important port of Pusan at the extreme southeastern corner of the peninsula. After violent fighting, a stable defense line was established. As American forces and contingents from fifteen other nations poured in, General Douglas MacArthur, Commander-in-Chief of U.S. forces in the Far East and Supreme Commander of the UN forces, decided on a daring amphibious landing at Inchon, a west coast port just a few miles from Seoul. The brilliantly conceived operation, launched on September 15, 1950, proved successful, and the North Korean Army, was forced to retreat back across the 38th parallel. Pressed by public demands for a complete victory, the Truman Administration gave General MacArthur the go-ahead to pursue the enemy across the demarcation line, justifying the decision with the UN Security Council's authorization. The first crossings took place on October 1. United Nations and ROK forces moved north, and by late November they were nearing the Yalu river boundary between North Korea and Communist China.

The seesaw struggle was reversed once again by the entry of Chinese "volunteers" into the war. Chinese leaders had warned that they would not allow North Korea to be invaded and would come to the aid of the North Koreans. By late October, thousands of Chinese soldiers had crossed the Yalu. One month later, they struck at the exposed flank and rear of

MacArthur's overextended armies. By early December, UN troops were again in headlong retreat, a withdrawal marked by great heroism but resulting in near disaster.

This created a crisis of the first order for President Truman. Truman wanted to stabilize the battle lines and negotiate an end to the war. General MacArthur wanted to attack China, possibly using tactical nuclear weapons. He said as much in a letter to House Republican leader Joseph W. Martins. Truman could not brook this challenge to his authority and, on April 11, 1951, he relieved MacArthur of command. Although the public clearly sided with MacArthur, Truman's strong stand settled the question of civilian control over the military.

A new battle line was organized south of the 38th parallel, and through the remaining winter and early spring months the lines fluctuated from south of Seoul to north of the parallel. Stalemate finally was achieved in July 1951. The conflict settled down to trench warfare, at which the Chinese were particularly adept, and was marked by indecisive but bloody fighting. This conflict lasted for two cruel years, during which time, more than a million Americans served in Korea.

For much of this period, talks proceeded at P'anmunjom, Korea near the 38th parallel. These talks opened on July 10, 1951 at the suggestion of the Communists. Welcomed by the most Americans, these negotiations were designed to achieve a cease-fire and an armistice. They were broken off repeatedly as germ warfare charges and difficulties over prisoner-of-war exchanges clouded the atmosphere.

The stalemate in Korea was a source of mounting frustration in the U.S., where it heightened the "red scare" and furnished ammunition to Senator Joseph McCarthy in his quest to purge leftists from the government and from influence in the society at large. The Korean War also helped elect Dwight D. Eisenhower to the Presidency. The Republican nominee won support by promising to go to Korea if elected. Eisenhower kept his pledge, but the visit had no noticeable effect on the peace talks.

The Communists finally modified their position on forcible repatriation of prisoners, and a final armistice agreement was signed at P'anmunjom on July 27, 1953. It resulted in a cease-fire and the withdrawal of both armies two kilometers from the battle line, which ran from coast to coast from just below the 38th parallel in the west to thirty miles north of it in the east. The agreement also provided for the creation of a Neutral Nations Supervisory Commission to carry out the terms of armistice. The armistice called for a political conference to settle all remaining questions, including the future of

Korea and the fate of prisoners who refused to return to their homelands. In succeeding months, the United Nations repatriated more than 70,000 North Korean and Communist prisoners but received in return only 3,597 Americans, 7,848 South Koreans, and 1,315 prisoners of other nationalities. The political conference was never held, and relations between North and South Korea remained hostile.

The Korean War cost the United States approximately 140,000 casualties including some 22,500 dead, and $22 billion. The results were somewhat inconclusive, but the war did prevent the Communist conquest of South Korea, and it demonstrated that the United States would fight to prevent the further spread of Communism. The war did change U.S. foreign policy. It marked a shift in military strategy from aiming for total victory to one of fighting limited wars.

The Korean police action also brought about a quick reversal of the policy of down-sizing the military. Major national security expenditures rapidly increased as a result of the war; national defense expenditures rose from four percent to 13 percent of gross national product in 1953. Defense spending revived inflationary impulses in the economy until the imposition of direct controls in January 1951 stabilized prices. In general, the Korean conflict changed the policy of containment from a selective European policy into a general global policy, and it contributed to the development of the military-industrial complex in America.

APPENDIX 16: "THE GREAT SOCIETY"

[Excerpts from "The Great Society." Gale Encyclopedia of U.S. Economic History. 1999. Retrieved 24 September 2013 from Encyclopedia.com: http:// www.encyclopedia.com/doc/1G2-3406400387.html]

The United States mourned when President John F. Kennedy (1960–1963) was assassinated on November 22, 1963....When Kennedy's Vice President, Lyndon B. Johnson (1963–1968) assumed the presidency, he pushed to make many of Kennedy's proposals into law. Capitalizing on U.S. stability, as well as the emotions of Kennedy's death, Johnson proposed anti-poverty, civil rights, education, and health care laws. In a speech at the University of Michigan in May 1964, Johnson said he hoped these programs would help create a "Great Society."

Great Society programs, as they came to be known, assisted millions, but they were very controversial. In the short run, funding for these costly programs decreased, as the United States spent more and more fighting the Vietnam War (1964–1975). In the long run, many critics have charged that these initiatives resulted in high taxes, "big government," and that they actually hurt the very people they were designed to help. Nonetheless, Great Society programs such as Medicare, which assists the elderly with medical expenses, remained popular and in the late 1990s they were still a crucial part of many Americans' lives.

Great Society programs were not the first large scale effort by the federal government to aid the disadvantaged. President Franklin D. Roosevelt (1932–1945) promised a "New Deal" to all Americans when he was elected. This "New Deal" was a long list of employment, income-assistance, and labor legislation, and it also had many critics.

But President Roosevelt's New Deal came at a time of mass poverty, when the United States and the world were living through the tough economic times of the Great Depression (1929–1939). Having emerged from World War II (1939–1945) as the world's most powerful nation, the United States experienced astounding economic growth in the 1950s and 1960s. Many Americans who barely had enough to eat during the Depression, now found themselves living in brand new homes and driving automobiles.

President Kennedy believed this national wealth could be used to uplift those who had not yet shared in the good economic times. Particularly disadvantaged were African Americans, who faced legal segregation in the South and poverty and discrimination in the North. In the tradition of

Roosevelt's New Deal, Kennedy proposed employment, education, and health care legislation. .

This was the legacy President Lyndon Johnson (1963–1969) hoped to fulfill with his Great Society. A masterful politician, Johnson may have lacked Kennedy's public grace, but he made up for it with political savvy. A former leader in the Senate, Johnson would need these skills to enact his ambitious programs which faced serious opposition in Congress.

During the summer of 1964 Johnson challenged Congress to pass the Economic Opportunity Act, the foundation for what came to be known as the "war on poverty." Johnson also proposed the Civil Rights Act of 1964, which combated racial discrimination. Johnson said enacting these bills would be a fitting tribute to Kennedy.

Johnson's initiatives seemed to be popular with voters. He won the 1964 election in a landslide. Capitalizing on what appeared to be a mandate from the American people, Johnson quickly proposed a wide range of programs for mass transportation, food stamps, immigration, and legal services for the poor. Bills aiding elementary, secondary, and higher education were also passed. Medicaid and Medicare were established to assist the poor and elderly, respectively, with medical treatment.

Other initiatives created the Department of Housing and Urban Development, aimed at improving housing conditions, particularly in crowded cities, and Project Head Start, which aided poor children in their earliest years of education. The National Endowment for the Humanities and the Corporation for Public Broadcasting were created in an effort to expand access to culture.

These programs cost billions of dollars but Johnson presented them not only as moral and just but also as a way to further expand the U.S. economy using education, job training, and income assistance. Johnson's party, the Democrats, won big again in the 1966 elections. However, forces were already converging, which would make it difficult to carry out Great Society programs. Across the country cities were exploding with demonstrations and even riots. Some wondered why problems seemed to be getting worse, just as billions of dollars had been committed to solving them.

A more daunting problem lay halfway around the world. The War in Vietnam claimed an increasing amount of Johnson's attention. And the war became just as controversial as Johnson's War on Poverty. It was also becoming more and more expensive as troops and supplies poured into the region to combat the "Viet Cong" guerilla fighters and the North Vietnamese Army. Johnson was pressured to hike taxes to cover the soaring costs of the war and his Great Society measures. Johnson's need for a tax increase gave political opponents leverage to demand domestic spending cuts. By 1968 Johnson's top economic and political priority was the increasingly unpopular war in Vietnam. This commitment ultimately led to him refusing to seek reelection as the Democratic presidential candidate.

That year also saw California Governor Ronald Reagan (1911–) fail in his bid to become the Republican presidential candidate. But twelve years later, when the nation's economy was stagnant, Reagan was elected president on a platform that identified many of Johnson's programs as the source of the nation's economic woes. Republicans like Reagan claimed the burden of Great Society initiatives on taxpayers had become too great while poverty only seemed to worsen. "It was 25 years ago that Lyndon Johnson announced his plans for 'The Great Society,'" the conservative magazine *National Review* wrote in 1989. "Today the phrase refers only to a bundle of welfare programs that have helped make the federal budget a chronic problem."

Republicans stepped up their attack into the 1990s and in 1994 they won majorities in both houses of Congress. They continued to criticize federal spending on programs such as Aid to Families with Dependent Children, more commonly called welfare, which were greatly expanded under the Great Society. Some Democrats said the attacks unfairly singled out society's most vulnerable citizens. Republicans argued that such social programs lead to dependency, which creates problems for both the beneficiary and the nation. Even President Bill Clinton (1993—), a Democrat, declared an "end to welfare as we know it."

Despite the criticism a diverse selection of Great Society programs, from Medicare to public television, remain politically popular. The ultimate legacy of the Great Society will surely be debated for decades to come.

APPENDIX 17: "THE VIETNAM WAR"

[Excerpts from "Vietnam War." Dictionary of American History. 2003. Retrieved 24 September 2013 from Encyclopedia.com: http://www.encyclopedia.com/doc/ 1G2-3401804406.html]

[The] Vietnam War, fought from 1957 until spring 1975, began as a struggle between the Republic of Vietnam (South Vietnam) supported by the United States and a Communist-led insurgency assisted by the Democratic Republic of Vietnam (North Vietnam)...both the United States and North Vietnam [eventually] committed their regular military forces to the struggle. North Vietnam received economic and military assistance from the Soviet Union and the People's Republic of China. The Republic of Korea, Australia, New Zealand, Thailand, and the Philippines furnished troops to the U.S.–South Vietnamese side. With 45,943 U.S. battle deaths, Vietnam was the fourth costliest war the country fought in terms of loss of life.

The Vietnam War was a continuation of the Indochina War of 1946–1954, in which the Communist dominated Vietnamese nationalists (Viet Minh) defeated France's attempt to reestablish colonial rule. American involvement began in 1950 when President Harry S. Truman invoked the Mutual Defense Assistance Act of 1949 to provide aid to French forces in Vietnam, Laos, and Cambodia. Early U.S. aims were to halt the spread of Communism and to encourage French participation in the international defense of Europe.

Even with U.S. aid in the form of materiel and a Military Assistance Advisory Group (MAAG), the French could not defeat the Viet Minh use of both guerrilla warfare and conventional attacks. Ending the Indochina War, the Geneva Accords of 1954 divided Vietnam at the seventeenth parallel with a three-mile Demilitarized Zone (DMZ). The partition in effect created two nations: the Democratic Republic of Vietnam in the north with its capital at Hanoi, and the Republic of Vietnam in the south with its capital at Saigon. Vietnam's neighbors, Laos and Cambodia, became independent nations under nominally neutralist governments.

The administration of President Dwight D. Eisenhower provided aid and support to the government of Ngo Dinh Diem. The MAAG, which grew in strength from 342 personnel to nearly 700, helped Diem to build up his armed forces. In 1956, with Eisenhower's concurrence, Diem refused to participate in the national elections called for in the Geneva Accords, asserting that South Vietnam had not acceded to the agreement and that free elections were impossible in the north, and declared himself president of the Republic of Vietnam.

During the first years of his rule, Diem, assisted by the MAAG, American civilian advisers, and by $190 million a year in U.S. financial aid, established effective armed forces and a seemingly stable government. He defeated or co-opted South Vietnamese rivals, resettled some 800,000 Catholic refugees from North Vietnam, initiated land reform, and conducted a campaign to wipe out the Viet Minh organization that remained in the south...Diem's regime was inefficient and riddled with corruption. Its land reform brought little benefit to the rural poor. Commanded by generals selected for loyalty to Diem rather than ability, the armed forces were poorly trained and low in morale. The anti–Viet Minh campaign alienated many peasants, and Diem's increasingly autocratic rule turned much of the urban anticommunist elite against him.

Anticipating control of South Vietnam through elections and preoccupied with internal problems, North Vietnam's charismatic leader, Ho Chi Minh, at first did little to exploit the vulnerabilities of the southern regime. Nevertheless, Ho and his colleagues were committed to the liberation of all of Vietnam and had accepted the Geneva Accords only with reluctance, under pressure from the Russians and Chinese, who hoped to avoid another Korea-type confrontation with the United States. In deference to his allies' caution and to American power, Ho moved slowly at the outset against South Vietnam.

Beginning in 1957, the southern Viet Minh, with authorization from Hanoi, launched a campaign of political subversion and terrorism, and gradually escalated a guerrilla war against Diem's government. Diem quickly gave the insurgents the label Viet Cong (VC), which they retained throughout the ensuing struggle. North Vietnam created a political organization in the south, the National Front for the Liberation of South Vietnam (NLF), ostensibly a broad coalition of elements opposed to Diem but controlled from the north by a Communist inner core. To reinforce the revived insurgency, Hanoi began sending southward soldiers and political cadres who had regrouped to North Vietnam after the armistice in 1954. These men, and growing quantities of weapons and equipment, traveled to South Vietnam via a network of routes through eastern Laos called the Ho Chi Minh Trail and by sea in junks and trawlers. At this stage, however, the vast majority of Viet Cong were native southerners, and they secured most of their weapons and supplies by capture from government forces.

Building on the organizational base left from the French war and exploiting popular grievances against Diem, the Viet Cong rapidly extended their political control of the countryside. Besides conducting small guerrilla operations, they gradually began to mount larger assaults with battalion and then regimental size light infantry units. As the fighting intensified, the first American deaths occurred in July 1959, when two soldiers of the MAAG were killed during a Viet Cong attack on Bien Hoa, north of Saigon. By the time President John F. Kennedy took office in 1961, it was clear that America's ally needed additional help.

Kennedy viewed the conflict in South Vietnam as a test case of Communist expansion by means of local "wars of national liberation." For that reason, as well as a continuing commitment to the general policy of "containment," Kennedy enlarged the U.S. effort in South Vietnam. He sent in more advisers to strengthen Diem's armed forces, provided additional funds and equipment, and deployed American helicopter companies and other specialized units. To carry out the enlarged program, Kennedy created a new joint (army, navy, air force) headquarters in Saigon, the Military Assistance Command, Vietnam (MACV). The number of Americans in South Vietnam increased to more than 16,000 and they began engaging in combat with the Viet Cong.

After a promising start, the Kennedy program faltered. Diem's dictatorial rule undermined South Vietnamese military effectiveness and fed popular discontent, especially among the country's numerous Buddhists. An effort to relocate the rural population in supposedly secure "strategic hamlets" collapsed due to poor planning and ineffective execution. With support from the Kennedy administration, Diem's generals overthrew and assassinated him in a coup d'etat on 1 November 1963.

Diem's death, followed by the assassination of President Kennedy on 22 November 1963, did nothing to improve allied fortunes. As a succession of unstable Saigon governments floundered, the Viet Cong began advancing from guerrilla warfare to larger attacks aimed at destroying the South Vietnamese Army (ARVN). To reinforce the campaign, Hanoi infiltrated quantities of modern Communist-bloc infantry weapons, and in late 1964, began sending units of its regular army into South Vietnam. Kennedy's successor, Lyndon B. Johnson, during 1964 increased American military manpower in South Vietnam to 23,300 and tried to revive the counterinsurgency campaign. However, political chaos in Saigon and growing Viet Cong strength in the countryside frustrated his efforts and those of the MACV commander, General William C. Westmoreland.

Johnson and his advisers turned to direct pressure on North Vietnam. Early in 1964, they initiated a program of small-scale covert raids on the north and began planning for air strikes. In August 1964, American planes raided North Vietnam in retaliation for two torpedo boat attacks (the second of which probably did not occur) on U.S. destroyers in the Gulf of Tonkin. Johnson used this incident to secure authorization from Congress (the Tonkin Gulf Resolution) to use armed force to "repel any armed attack against the forces of the United States and to repel further aggression." That resolution served as a legal basis for subsequent increases in the U.S. commitment, but in 1970 after questions arose as to whether the administration had misrepresented the incidents, Congress repealed it.

Committed like his predecessors to containment and to countering Communist "wars of national liberation," Johnson also wanted to maintain U.S. credibility as an ally and feared the domestic political repercussions of losing South Vietnam. Accordingly, he and his advisers moved toward further escalation.

During 1964, Johnson authorized limited U.S. bombing of the Ho Chi Minh Trail. In February 1965, after the Viet Cong killed thirty-one Americans at Pleiku and Qui Nhon, the President sanctioned retaliatory strikes against North Vietnam. In March, retaliation gave way to a steadily intensified but carefully controlled aerial offensive against the north (Operation Rolling Thunder), aimed at reducing Hanoi's ability to support the Viet Cong and compelling its leaders to negotiate an end to the conflict on U.S. terms.

At the same time, Johnson committed American combat forces to the fight. Seven U.S. Marine battalions and an Army airborne brigade entered South Vietnam between March and May 1965. Their initial mission was to defend air bases used in Operation Rolling Thunder, but in April, Johnson expanded their role to active operations against the Viet Cong. During the same period, Johnson authorized General Westmoreland to employ U.S. jets in combat in the south, and in June, B-52 strategic bombers began raiding Viet Cong bases. As enemy pressure on the ARVN continued and evidence accumulated that North Vietnamese regular divisions were entering the battle, Westmoreland called for a major expansion of the ground troop commitment. On 28 July, Johnson announced deployments that would bring U.S. strength to 180,000 by the end of 1965. Westmoreland threw these troops into action against the Viet Cong and North Vietnamese's large military units. Taking advantage of their helicopter-borne mobility, U.S. forces won early tactical victories, but the cost in American dead and wounded also began to mount and the enemy showed no signs of backing off.

Additional deployments increased American troop strength to a peak of 543,400 by 1969. To support them, MACV, using troops and civilian engineering firms, constructed or expanded ports, erected fortified camps, built vast depots, paved thousands of miles of roads, and created a network of airfields.

Desiring to keep the war limited to Vietnam, President Johnson authorized only small-scale raids into the enemy bases in Laos and Cambodia. As a result, in South Vietnam, General Westmoreland perforce fought a war of attrition. He used his American troops to battle the North Vietnamese and Viet Cong regular units while the ARVN and South Vietnam's territorial forces carried on the pacification campaign against the Viet Cong guerrillas and political infrastructure. As the fighting went on, a stable government emerged in Saigon under Nguyen Van Thieu. These efforts, however, brought only stalemate. Aided by Russia and China, the North Vietnamese countered Operation Rolling Thunder with an air defense system of increasing sophistication and effectiveness. In South Vietnam, they fed in troops to match the American buildup and engaged in their own campaign of attrition. While suffering heavier losses than the U.S. in most engagements, they inflicted a steady and rising toll of American dead. Pacification in South Vietnam made little progress. The fighting produced South Vietnamese civilian casualties, the result of enemy terrorism, American bombing and shelling, and in a few instances—notably the My Lai massacre of March 1968—of atrocities by U.S. troops.

In the U.S., opposition to the war grew to encompass a broad spectrum of the public even as doubts about America's course emerged within the administration. By the end of 1967, President Johnson had decided to level off the bombing in the north and American troop strength in the south and to seek a way out of the war, possibly by turning more of the fighting over to the South Vietnamese.

Late in 1967, North Vietnam's leaders decided to break what they also saw as a stalemate by conducting a "General Offensive/General Uprising," a combination of heavy military attacks with urban revolts. After preliminary battles, the North Vietnamese early in 1968 besieged a Marine base at Khe Sanh in far northwestern South Vietnam. On the night of 31 January, during the Tet (Lunar New Year) holidays, 84,000 enemy troops attacked seventy-four towns and cities including Saigon. Although U.S. intelligence had gleaned something of the plan, the extent of the attacks on the cities came as a surprise.

Viet Cong units initially captured portions of many towns, but they failed to spark a popular uprising. Controlling Hué for almost a month, they executed 3,000 civilians as "enemies of the people." ARVN and U.S. troops quickly cleared most localities, and the besiegers of Khe Sanh withdrew after merciless pounding by American air power and artillery. At the cost of 32,000 dead (by MACV estimate), the Tet Offensive produced no lasting enemy military advantage.

In the United States, however, the Tet Offensive confirmed President Johnson's determination to wind down the war. Confronting bitter antiwar dissent within the Democratic Party and a challenge to his renomination from Senator Eugene McCarthy, Johnson rejected a military request for additional U.S. troops and halted most bombing of the north. He also withdrew from the presidential race to devote the rest of his term to the search for peace in Vietnam. In return for the partial bombing halt, North Vietnam agreed to open negotiations. Starting in Paris in May 1968, the talks were unproductive for a long time.

Taking office in 1969, President Richard M. Nixon continued the Paris talks. He also began withdrawing U.S. troops from South Vietnam while simultaneously building up Saigon's forces so that they could fight on with only American advice and materiel assistance. This program was labeled "Vietnamization."

Because the Viet Cong had been much weakened by its heavy losses in the Tet Offensive and in two subsequent general offensives in May and August 1968, the years 1969–1971 witnessed apparent allied progress in South Vietnam. The ARVN gradually took on the main burden of the ground fighting, which declined in intensity. American troop strength diminished from its 1969 peak of 543,400 to 156,800 at the end of 1971. The allies also made progress in pacification. American and South Vietnamese offensives against the enemy sanctuaries in Cambodia in April and May 1970 and an ARVN raid against the Ho Chi Minh Trail in February 1971 helped to buy time for Vietnamization. On the negative side, as a result of trends in American society, of disillusionment with the war among short-term draftee soldiers, and of organizational turbulence caused by the troop withdrawals, U.S. forces suffered from growing indiscipline, drug abuse, and racial conflict.

In spring 1972, North Vietnam, in order to revive its fortunes in the south, launched the so-called Easter Offensive with twelve divisions, employing tanks and artillery on a scale not previously seen in the war. In response, President Nixon, while he continued to withdraw America's remaining ground troops, increased U.S. air support to the ARVN. The North Vietnamese made initial territorial gains, but the ARVN rallied, assisted materially by U.S. Air Force and Navy planes and American advisers on the ground. Meanwhile, Nixon resumed full-scale bombing of North Vietnam and mined its harbors. Beyond defeating the Easter Offensive, Nixon intended these attacks, which employed B-52s and technologically advanced guided bombs, to batter Hanoi toward a negotiated settlement of the war. By late 1972, the North Vietnamese, had lost an estimated 100,000 dead and large amounts of equipment and had failed to capture any major towns or populated areas. Nevertheless, their military position in the south was better than it had been in 1971, and the offensive had facilitated a limited revival of the Viet Cong.

Both sides were ready for a negotiated settlement. During the autumn of 1972, Nixon's special adviser, Henry A. Kissinger, and North Vietnamese representative Le Duc Tho, who had been negotiating in secret since 1969, reached the outlines of an agreement. Each side made a key concession. The U.S. dropped its demand for complete withdrawal of North Vietnamese troops from South Vietnam. Hanoi abandoned its insistence that the Thieu government be replaced by a presumably Communist-dominated coalition. After additional diplomatic maneuvering between Washington and Hanoi and Washington and Saigon, which balked at the terms, and after a final U.S. air campaign against Hanoi in December, the ceasefire agreement went into effect on 28 January 1973.

Under it, military prisoners were returned, all American troops withdrew, and a four-nation commission supervised the truce. In fact, the fighting in South Vietnam continued, and the elections called for in the agreement never took place. During 1973 and 1974, the North Vietnamese, in violation of the ceasefire, massed additional men and supplies inside South Vietnam. Meanwhile, the Nixon administration, distracted by the Watergate scandal, had to accept a congressional cutoff of all funds for American combat operations in Southeast Asia after 15 August 1973.

Early in 1975, the North Vietnamese, again employing regular divisions with armor and artillery, launched their final offensive against South Vietnam. That nation, exhausted by years of fighting, demoralized by a steady reduction in the flow of American aid, and lacking capable leadership at the top, rapidly collapsed. A misguided effort by President Thieu to regroup his forces in northern South Vietnam set off a rout that continued almost unbroken until the North Vietnamese closed in on Saigon late in April. On 21 April, President Thieu resigned. His successor, General Duong Van Minh, surrendered the country on 30 April. North Vietnamese and Viet Cong troops entered Saigon only hours after the U.S. completed an emergency airlift of embassy personnel and thousands of South Vietnamese who feared for their lives under the Communists. Hanoi gained control of South Vietnam, and its allies won in Cambodia, where the government surrendered to insurgent forces on 17 April 1975, and Laos, where the Communists gradually assumed control.

The costs of the war were high for every participant. Besides combat deaths, the U.S. lost 1,333 men missing and 10,298 dead of non-battle causes. In terms of money ($138.9 billion), only World War II was more expensive. Costs less tangible but equally real were the loss of trust by American citizens in their government and the demoralization of the U.S. armed forces, which would take years to recover their discipline and self-confidence. South Vietnam suffered more than 166,000 military dead and possibly as many as 415,000 civilians. North Vietnamese and Viet Cong deaths amounted to at least 937,000. To show for the effort, the U.S. could claim only that it had delayed South Vietnam's fall long enough for other Southeast Asian countries to stabilize their noncommunist governments.

APPENDIX 18: "THE REAGAN DOCTRINE"

[Excerpts from Brinkley, Alan. "Reagan, Ronald." Presidents: A Reference History. 2002. Retrieved 26 December from http://www.encyclopedia.com/topic/ Ronald_Wilson_Reagan.aspx#1]

[The administration of President Ronald W. Reagan] began—rhetorically at least—to support forces opposing Communism almost anywhere in the world, whether or not the regimes or movements such forces were challenging had any direct connection to the Soviet Union. This new policy became known as the Reagan Doctrine, and it represented a conscious effort to repudiate the lessons that liberals and others had drawn from the failed war in Vietnam. Reagan called Vietnam a "noble cause," and both he and his supporters seemed to believe that the American defeat had been more the result of insufficient resolve than of the flawed premises of the original commitment. In practice, the Reagan Doctrine meant above all a new American activism in Latin America. In October 1983, the administration sent American soldiers into the tiny Caribbean island of Grenada to oust an anti-American Marxist regime that showed signs of forging a relationship with Moscow. In El Salvador, where first a repressive military regime and later a moderate civilian one were engaged in murderous struggles with left-wing revolutionaries (who were supported, according to the Reagan administration, by Cuba and the Soviet Union), the president provided increased military and economic assistance. In neighboring Nicaragua, a pro-American dictatorship had fallen to the revolutionary Sandinistas in 1979; the new government had grown increasingly anti-American (and increasingly Marxist) throughout the early 1980s. The administration gave both rhetorical and material support to the so-called contras, a guerrilla movement drawn from several anti-government groups and fighting (without great success) to topple the Sandinista regime. Indeed, support of the contras became a mission of special importance to the president, and later the source of some of his greatest difficulties.

In other parts of the world, the administration's bellicose public statements masked an instinctive restraint. In June 1982, the Israeli army launched an invasion of Lebanon in an effort to drive guerrillas of the Palestine Liberation Organization from the country. The United States supported the Israelis but also worked to permit PLO forces to leave Lebanon peacefully. An American peace-keeping force entered Beirut to supervise the evacuation. American marines then remained in the city, apparently to protect the fragile Lebanese government, which was embroiled in a vicious civil war. Now identified with one faction in the struggle, Americans became the targets in 1983 of a terrorist bombing of a U.S. military barracks in

Beirut that left 241 marines dead. Rather than become more deeply involved in the Lebanese struggle, Reagan withdrew American forces.

The tragedy in Lebanon was an example of the changing character of many Third World struggles: an increasing reliance on terrorism by otherwise powerless groups to advance their political aims. A series of terrorist acts in the 1980s—attacks on airplanes, cruise ships, commercial and diplomatic posts; the seizing of American and European hostages—alarmed and frightened much of the Western world. The Reagan administration spoke bravely about its resolve to punish terrorism; and at one point in 1986, the president ordered American planes to bomb sites in Tripoli, the capital of Libya, whose controversial leader Mu'ammar al-Gadhafi was widely believed to be a leading sponsor of terrorism. In general, however, terrorists remained difficult to identify or control; and the administration's private resolve in the face of terrorism was never as firm as its public rhetoric suggested.

....Shortly after Reagan took his oath of office for the second time...a new leader took power in the Soviet Union: Mikhail S. Gorbachev, who was, by Soviet standards at least, a young and energetic head of state. In the beginning, American leaders expected little from Gorbachev. He had, after all, been molded by the same stultifying political system that had shaped his recent predecessors. But to the surprise of almost everyone (including, it sometimes seemed, himself), Gorbachev very quickly became the most revolutionary figure in world politics since the end of World War II. Benefiting from widespread frustration with the rigid and ineffective policies of the preceding twenty years, Gorbachev transformed Soviet politics with two dramatic new initiatives. The first he called glasnost (openness). Glasnost led to the dismantling of many of the repressive mechanisms that had been among the most conspicuous features of Soviet life for more than half a century. Gradually it became possible for Soviet citizens to express themselves more freely, to criticize the government, even to organize politically in opposition to official policy. The other initiative Gorbachev called perestroika (reform or restructuring). Through it, he attempted to remake the rigid and unproductive Soviet economy by introducing, among other things, such elements of capitalism as private ownership and the profit motive. At the same time, Gorbachev began reshaping Soviet foreign policy. Among the first steps in that effort was his attempt to forge a new relationship with the United States.

He began by reaching out to Washington for major new arms control agreements. Encouraged by British prime minister Margaret Thatcher, a friend and ideological ally of Reagan's and an early champion of Gorbachev's, Reagan too began looking for new avenues to accommodation. At a summit meeting with Reagan in Reykjavfk, Iceland, in 1986 (the second of four between the two leaders), Gorbachev proposed reducing the nuclear arsenals of both sides by 50 percent or more. Continuing disputes over Reagan's commitment to the SDI program, among other things, prevented agreements. But in December 1987, after Reagan and Gorbachev exchanged cordial visits to each other's capitals, the two leaders signed a treaty eliminating American and Soviet intermediate-range nuclear forces (INF) from Europe—the most significant arms control agreement of the nuclear age and the first to make actual reductions in existing nuclear arsenals as opposed to restricting their future expansion. At about the same time, Gorbachev ended the Soviet Union's long and frustrating military involvement in Afghanistan, removing one of the principal irritants in the relationship between Washington and Moscow.

The new arms control agreements, and the rapid moderation of Soviet international behavior, seemed to Reagan and his supporters a clear vindication of the president's earlier policies. By increasing diplomatic and economic pressure on the Soviet Union, and in particular by forcing the Soviets into an expensive new arms race that their staggering economy could not support, the administration had done much to weaken the hard-liners in Moscow and make Gorbachev's reforms possible, even likely. (Reagan had always claimed that the arms buildup he launched was designed, at least in part, to encourage the Soviet Union to agree to arms reductions.) Others were more skeptical and insisted that the decay of the Soviet Union had begun long before Reagan's presidency and had intensified for reasons that had little to do with American policy. In either case, Reagan—a hard-line foe of Soviet Communism for more than forty years—proved flexible enough to respond to the changes and encourage them.

For a time, the dramatic developments around the world and Reagan's continuing personal popularity deflected attention from a series of scandals that might well have destroyed another administration. Top officials in the Environmental Protection Agency resigned when it was disclosed that they were flouting the laws they had been appointed to enforce. Officials of the CIA and the Defense Department resigned after revelations of questionable stock transactions. Reagan's secretary of labor, Raymond J. Donovan, left office after being indicted for racketeering (although he was later acquitted). Edwin Meese, the White House counsel and later attorney general, finally resigned in 1988 after years of controversy over financial arrangements that many believed had compromised his office.

Unnoticed at first were several larger scandals that surfaced only as Reagan was about to leave office. One involved misuse of funds by the

Department of Housing and Urban Development, abuses so widespread that by 1990 the survival of the agency itself seemed in question. Another, more serious scandal involved the savings and loan industry. The Reagan administration had sharply reduced regulatory controls over the troubled savings and loan institutions, permitting them to enter into business activities from which they had previously been barred. Many savings banks responded by rapidly, often recklessly, and sometimes corruptly, expanding. By the end of the decade the industry was in chaos, and the government was forced to step in to prevent a complete collapse. The government insured the assets of most savings and loan depositors; and as the banks failed, it found itself saddled with large debts. The eventual cost of the debacle to the public ran to more than half a trillion dollars.

But the most politically damaging scandal of the Reagan years came to light in November 1986. After reports of the episode had begun appearing in foreign newspapers, the White House conceded that it had sold weapons to the revolutionary government of Iran, apparently as part of a largely unsuccessful effort to secure the release of several Americans being held hostage by radical Islamic groups in the Middle East. Even more damaging was the administration's admission that some of the money from the arms deal with Iran had been covertly and illegally funneled into a fund to aid the contras in Nicaragua.

In the months that followed, aggressive reporting and a highly publicized series of congressional hearings exposed a remarkable and previously un-suspected feature of the Reagan White House: the existence within it of something like a "secret government," largely unknown to the State Department, the Defense Department, even parts of the CIA, dedicated to advancing the administration's foreign policy aims through secret and at times illegal means. The principal figure in this covert world appeared at first to be an obscure marine lieutenant colonel assigned to the staff of the National Security Council, Oliver L. North. But gradually it became clear that North was acting in concert with other, more powerful figures in the administration: two national security advisers, Robert McFarlane and John M. Poindexter and, many believed, both the vice president and the president himself....

APPENDIX 19: "THE GULF WAR"

[Excerpts from Cannon, John. "Gulf War." The Oxford Companion to British History. 2002. Retrieved 26 December 2013 from Encyclopedia.com: http:// www.encyclopedia.com/doc/1O110-GulfWar.html]

....On 2 August 1990 Iraq invaded the tiny neighbouring state of Kuwait, giving the Iraqi dictator Saddam Hussein control of about 15 per cent of the world's oil, with a threat to a further 25 per cent. The almost defunct Soviet Union (which collapsed in December 1991) did not block a strong American response, which employed the United Nations Security Council to denounce Iraq's action and won Saudi Arabian agreement to receive large American forces. In response, on 8 August, Iraq announced the incorporation of Kuwait into Iraq, an act of direct conquest unprecedented among United Nations members.

President George Bush portrayed American military action as the start of a 'New World Order' following the end of the Cold War. Bush assembled a coalition of twenty-nine countries against Iraq, although with its immense armed forces and technological superiority the USA dominated the coalition in all respects. Britain's policy was to support the USA completely, to demonstrate both her reliability as an ally and her importance as a second-ranking power. By stripping her armed forces Britain contributed small but significant naval, air, and ground units to the war, all closely subordinated to American command.

The coalition forces took several months to assemble in Saudi Arabia. Iraqi strategy was to prevent a coalition forming by playing on pan-Arab sentiment, in particular over past American support for Israel. On 29 November the United Nations Security Council set a deadline of 15 January 1991 for Iraqi withdrawal from Kuwait, authorizing the use of force ('all necessary means') to support this.

Early on 17 January 1991, the coalition began with a massive air bombing attack against Iraq, which responded by attacking Israel (which was not a coalition member and had taken no military action) with long-range missiles. Critically for coalition solidarity, Israel refused to retaliate. The coalition launched its ground offensive to clear Kuwait on 24 February. This revealed that the Americans had greatly overestimated the Iraqi army, which virtually disintegrated, offering only token resistance. On 28 February, having achieved the objective of liberating Kuwait, Bush called a unilateral cease-fire, and a permanent cease-fire came into effect on 11 April.

With the liberation of Kuwait dissident groups within Iraq, notably the Kurds of the north, rose in rebellion. Over the next year Saddam gradually reasserted his rule, and survived in power. Ironically, Prime Minister Margaret Thatcher, who had first committed Britain to the coalition, was forced from office in November 1990, and Bush failed to gain re-election in 1992. ...the Gulf War secured oil supplies for the West, effectively destroyed Saddam's ambitions for Iraq as a regional power, and upheld the rule of law through the United Nations...

APPENDIX 20: "NAFTA"

[Excerpts from Schechter, Michael G.. "NAFTA (North American Free Trade Agreement)." Pollution A to Z. 2004. Retrieved September 25, 2013 from Encyclopedia.com: http://www.encyclopedia.com/doc/1G2-3408100169.html]

On December 17, 1992, Canada, Mexico, and the United States entered into a historical trade pact called the North American Free Trade Agreement (NAFTA). It aims to increase trade by expanding market access and reducing investment barriers across North American borders....A number of issues including labor market disruptions fueled intense debate over NAFTA, especially in the United States. But no issue received as much attention as the impact of NAFTA on the environment. Debate focused on (1) possible threats posed to previously signed U.S. domestic environmental laws and international environmental agreements; (2) concern that harmonization of environmental standards would result in acceptance of the least common denominator; and (3) fear that U.S. industries would establish pollution havens in Mexico, where labor is cheaper and enforcement of regulations is weaker than in the United States.

In order to allay such concerns, several provisions were added to the NAFTA text. For example, the preamble commits governments to undertake increased trade in "a manner consistent with environmental protection and conservation," and the agreement's dispute-settlement provisions can place the burden on the country challenging an environmental regulation. In addition, prior to NAFTA entering into force on January 1, 1994, the participating governments agreed to the North American Agreement on Environmental Cooperation (NAAEC), which obliges each country to "ensure that its laws and regulations provide for high levels of environmental protection and to strive to continue to improve those laws and regulations." It also ensures access by private persons to fair and equitable administrative and judicial proceedings on matters pertaining to the environment. The NAAEC established the Commission for Environmental Cooperation (CEC), which has three institutional components: a Council, a Secretariat, and a Joint Public Advisory Committee. The Council, assisted by the Secretariat, is charged with monitoring NAFTA's environmental impacts. When they uncover adverse environmental impacts, they publicize them in various ways, including posting notices on their web site. The aim of the council is that, by means of this public shaming, countries will take action to remedy these situations.

APPENDIX 21: "IRAQ WAR"

[Excerpts from Lerner, K. Lee "Iraq War (Immediate Aftermath)." Encyclopedia of Espionage, Intelligence, and Security. 2004. Retrieved 25 September 2013 from Encyclopedia.com: http://www.encyclopedia.com/doc/1G2-3403300414.html]

On May 1, 2003, United States President George W. Bush announced an end to major military combat operations related to Operation Iraqi Freedom.

Although evidence of Saddam Hussein's reign of terror was rapidly forthcoming—including the discovery of numerous mass gravesites of those brutally executed for resisting Hussein's rule—the anticipated discovery of large caches of Iraqi weapons of mass destruction (WMD) proved elusive. By the end of May 2003, both British and American intelligence agencies began to downplay the possibility of finding large stores of such weapons. ...questions remained as to whether the weapons had been removed, destroyed, or whether intelligence reports regarding the weapons had been mishandled, exaggerated, or falsified.

Although some seized on the growing controversy regarding the lack of WMD finds as a partisan political issue, all Western intelligence agencies, including those of war dissenter nations France and Germany, agreed before the war that Hussein's regime possessed weapons of mass destruction.

Attention in America and Europe focused on to what degree claims regarding Iraqi WMD programs might have been exaggerated, or as the British Broadcasting Corporation (BBC) reported, "sexed up" by both the Bush and Blair administrations to gain support for the war.

At the core of the controversy lay the handling of critical reports compiled by British intelligence regarding Hussein's possession and potential use of weapons of mass destruction. One report, publicly released by the British in 2002, asserted that Hussein's "military planning allows for some weapons of mass destruction to be ready within 45 minutes of an order to use them." This statement was used by Coalition governments to stress the urgency of war. Another report, also compiled by British intelligence and released just weeks before the start of military operations, allegedly had new intelligence information, but was subsequently exposed to contain material plagiarized from a previously published academic source.

A BBC report in late May 2003, alleged that a senior British official involved in the preparation of the Fall, 2002 report (containing claims regarding

Iraq's ability to rapidly assemble and use biological and chemical weapons) claimed that the report was rewritten on the instructions of officials in the administration of British Prime Minister Tony Blair to make it "sexier" (i.e., to stress the urgency of war). The BBC described their source as one of a number of senior British officials in charge of drawing up the report.

Officials in the Blair government, including John Scarlett, head of the Joint Intelligence Committee, countered that the report was entirely the work product of the intelligence community and that no pressure had been exerted to change its contents. Blair administration officials demanded a retraction and apology from the BBC. The BBC refused and stood by its story. Other British government officials initially characterized the BBC sources as "rogue elements within the intelligence services" who were against the government.

The British House of Commons foreign affairs committee began a series of hearings into the controversy and took statements from government officials and journalists regarding the BBC report. As of July 2003, the committee's initial conclusion was there was insufficient evidence of "improper influence," but that there was sufficient evidence to conclude that parts of the reports regarding Iraqi weapons readiness were given unwarranted emphasis. The committee specifically concluded that Alastair Campbell, the Blair administration's director of communications—specifically identified in BBC reports as one administration official who tried to influence report content—was not responsible for attempting to influence the contents of the report.

Another inquiry was led by the British Intelligence and Security Committee. During their hearings, testimony was provided by David Kelly, a government weapons expert. Although the BBC initially protected the identity of its source, following Kelly's death the BBC acknowledged that Kelly was the "principal source" for its claim that the report had been "sexed-up."

After the BBC aired its story in late May 2003, other news organizations sought the source of the BBC information and Kelly's name became publicly identified as the potential source of the BBC story. In July 2003, Kelly initially confirmed meeting with a BBC reporter, but denied he was the main source for the BBC report. Intense scrutiny along with and criticism of Kelly and his potential role in the story circulated in both press and government circles. Kelly blamed U.K. Ministry of Defense officials and others in the Blair government for leaking his name to the press. Kelly claimed that he was put under "intolerable" pressure by the disclosure of his association with the potential intelligence scandal.

Kelly went missing on July 17, 2003, and the next day his body was discovered near his Oxfordshire home with a knife and a packet of painkillers close to his body. Police confirmed that subsequent forensic examination concluded that Kelly committed suicide and bled to death from cuts to his wrist. Prime Minister Blair confirmed that there would be a judicial inquiry dealing with the events surrounding Kelly's death.

In July, 2003, U.S. Director of Central Intelligence, George Tenet accepted the blame for allowing subsequently discredited information from British Intelligence—that Hussein's government "recently sought significant quantities of uranium from Africa"—to remain in the text of President Bush's January 2003 State of the Union speech. Tenet acknowledged that the CIA had doubted the validity of the reports and that the evidence did not rise to the "level of certainty" normally required for insertion into presidential speeches.

At the end of July 2003, several inquires were underway into the formulation and use by Coalition governments of intelligence related to Iraqi possession and development of weapons of mass destruction.

The hunt for Hussein's regime. Against steady sniper and terrorist attacks, Coalition forces continued the hunt for former officials of Saddam Hussein's regime.

In July 2003, U.S. Army soldiers and Task Force 20 personnel (a special unit tasked with capturing or killing former Iraqi leaders) surrounded and killed Qusay and Uday Hussein, Saddam Hussein's sons and top officials of the former Iraqi régime. Following their discovery in Mosul, the former Iraqi leaders refused to surrender and an intense firefight ended in their deaths. U.S. officials debated and then released photos of the bodies, in part, to alleviate Iraqi fears that the two might still be alive and attempt a return to power. U.S. officials also hoped that the confirmation of the deaths of Qusay and Uday would encourage Iraqis to come forward with intelligence related to capturing Saddam.

As of July 30, 2003, Coalition forces and Task Force 20 had killed or captured almost 40 former Iraqi leaders depicted in a famous deck of playing cards sometimes dubbed the "deck of death," circulated to Coalition forces to assist them in spotting wanted former Iraqi leaders.

At the end of July, 2003, U.S. Central Command confirmed the deaths of 90 American service personnel killed in Iraq since President Bush's May 1 declaration of an end to major combat operations. At least 49 of those soldiers were killed in combat.

Books especially for the AP and IB student by Dr. Juan R. Céspedes.
Available on Amazon, Kindle, and other fine book emporiums.

The IB History Internal Assessment: An "A+" in 6 Easy Steps

101 IB History Exam-related Questions: ...and their answers!

The IB Extended Essay: An "A+" in 6 Easy Steps!

IB History Exam Study Guide: International Contemporary History 1848-2008

The Myopic Vision: The Causes of Totalitarianism, Authoritarianism, & Statism (Papers 1 & 2)

Collapse of the Soviet Empire: A Preparation for the International Baccalaureate History Examination (Papers 1 & 2)

War Interminable: The Origins, Causes, Practices and Effects of International Conflict (Papers 2 & 3)

The IB Extended Essay: An "A+" in 6 Easy Steps!

The IB History Internal Assessment: An A+ in 6 East Steps

About the Author

Dr. Juan R. Céspedes is a veteran educator, lecturer, and author. For nearly three decades Dr. Céspedes has shared his thoughts and research about history, politics, economics, and international relations with a wide audience. His many books include "Collapse of the Soviet Empire", an analysis of the communism in Europe and Eurasia, "War Interminable: The Origins, Causes, Practices and Effects of International Conflict", the "IB History Exam Study Guide: International Contemporary History 1848-2008", and recently "The Myopic Vision: The Causes of Totalitarianism, Authoritarianism, and Statism". An advocate of maximizing individual freedom, human dignity and democratic government, he has traveled widely, researched, and reported extensively on major topics such as the nature of totalitarian regimes, the Cold War, the causes of wars, and the history of terrorism. Dr. Céspedes is an Examiner for the International Baccalaureate Organization, a Social Studies test bank writer for the Florida Department of Education, and an Adjunct Professor at Florida International University's School of International and Public Affairs in the Gordon Institute for Public Policy and Citizenship Studies, where he teaches a course on the 20th century and contemporary issues.

Printed in the USA
CPSIA information can be obtained
at www.ICGtesting.com
LVHW042259240124
769917LV00006B/131